PIANO AEROBICS

Audio Access Included

BY WA

A Multi-Style, **40-Week** Workout Program for Building Real-World Technique

To access audio visit:
www.halleonard.com/mylibrary
Enter Code
5313-3787-1867-9356

Edited by Jennifer Linn

Cover Illustration by Birck Cox

ISBN 978-1-4234-7354-1

HAL•LEONARD®
7777 W. BLUEMOUND RD. P.O. BOX 13819 MILWAUKEE, WI 53213

In Australia Contact:
Hal Leonard Australia Pty. Ltd.
4 Lentara Court
Cheltenham, Victoria, 3192 Australia
Email: ausadmin@halleonard.com.au

Copyright © 2011 by HAL LEONARD CORPORATION
International Copyright Secured   All Rights Reserved

No part of this publication may be reproduced in any form
or by any means without the prior written permission of the Publisher.

Visit Hal Leonard Online at
www.halleonard.com

Table of Contents

		Page	Track
	Notes from the Author	1	
	How to Use This Book and Play-along Tracks	1	
Introduction			
	Hand Position	2	
	Warm-Up and Stretching Exercises	3	
Weeks 1-2	Keeping Time While Building Strength	5	
	Use of Metronome	5	
	Finger Strengthening Exercise	5	
	Finger Strengthening Workout #1	6	1
Weeks 3-4	Working with the Left Hand	9	
	What is Swing?	9	
	Left Hand Development	10	
	Boogie Woogie Workout	11	2
Weeks 5-6	Playing Independently	13	
	How to Use the Damper (Sustain) Pedal	13	
	Pedal Exercises	14	
	New Age Workout #1	15	3
Weeks 7-8	Articulations	18	
	Interpreting Articulations	18	
	Articulation Exercises	18	
	Articulation Workout	19	4
Weeks 9-10	Playing Rock Piano	22	
	Wrist Articulations	22	
	Wrist Exercises	22	
	Rock Workout	23	5
Weeks 11-12	Basic Blues	26	
	Thinking (But Not Always Seeing) Triplets	26	
	Blues Exercises	27	
	Blues Workout	28	6
Weeks 13-14	Building a Better Touch	31	
	The Importance of Touch	31	
	Hand and Finger Balancing	31	
	Touch Workout	32	7
Weeks 15-16	Strengthening Weak Fingers	36	
	Isolating and Strengthening Weak Fingers	36	
	Individual Finger Exercises	37	
	Finger Strengthening Workout #2	38	8
Weeks 17-18	Bossa Nova	41	
	Introduction to the Style	41	
	Rhythmic Syncopation Exercises	41	
	Bossa Nova Workout	42	9

		Page	Track
Weeks 19-20	Accompanying	46	
	Rhythm Playing versus Solo Playing	46	
	Vertical Reading Exercises	46	
	Vertical Reading Workout	47	10
Weeks 21-22	Use of the Thumb	51	
	All (About) Thumbs	51	
	Turning Exercises, Scales	51	
	(All) Thumbs Workout	52	11
Weeks 23-24	Relationship Between Blues and Jazz	56	
	Comparisons Between Blues and Jazz	56	
	Blues Exercise	57	
	Blues and Jazz Workout	58	12
Weeks 25-26	Salsa Piano	63	
	Intro to Salsa Jazz Piano	63	
	Son-Montuno Exercise	63	
	Salsa Workout	64	13
Weeks 27-28	Gospel Piano	68	
	The Backbeat	68	
	Harmonizing Scale Tones	68	
	Gospel Workout	69	14
Weeks 29-30	Four-Hand Piano Duets	73	
	Questions to Consider	73	
	Special Challenge	73	
	New Age Workout #2 (Duet)	74	15-17
Weeks 31-32	Jazz Piano	81	
	Intro to Swing and Bebop	81	
	Jazz Exercises	81	
	Modern Jazz Workout	82	18
Weeks 33-34	Ear Training	86	
	The Importance of Ear Training	86	
	Interval Training Exercises	86	
	Ear Training Workout (Call and Response)	87	19
Weeks 35-37	Brazilian Jazz	88	
	Brazilian Jazz Piano	88	
	Brazilian Jazz Exercises	88	
	Samba Workout	89	20
Weeks 38-40	Stride Piano	92	
	Use of the Left Hand in Ragtime and Jazz	92	
	Stride Exercises	92	
	Stride Workout	93	21

Acknowledgments

I would like to thank all of the students and musicians who have influenced me; my editor Jennifer Linn; my wife Sylvia Stoner-Hawkins and daughter Halina; and my grandmother Verna Baska who made me practice.

Wayne Hawkins

Recording

All piano and keyboards by Wayne Hawkins.
Luiz Orsano, Drums and Percussion
Forest Stewart, Electric Bass
Sam Wiseman, Drums
Anfrisio Rocha, Electric Bass, Nylon String Guitar, Cavaquinho
Aaron Simcox, Tenor Sax, Flute
Doug Talley, Tenor Sax
Tim Brewer, Acoustic Bass
Keith Kavanaugh, Drums

All Tracks were recorded in May 2011 at Healing Studios in Kansas City, Kansas. Luiz Orsano was the recording, mixing and mastering engineer.

Notes from the Author

When I was asked to write *Piano Aerobics*, I immediately thought about what I could contribute to the wealth of material already published. I wanted to create a set of exercises that students would enjoy playing.

Often when students decide to play contemporary styles of music, they lack the "chops" for the job.

Most traditional piano training has resulted in good interpretation and understanding of classical repertoire only. *Piano Aerobics* is a set of exercises that introduces students to many popular styles of music including Jazz, Salsa, Swing, Rock, Blues, New age, Gospel, Stride and Bossa Nova. Not only will these exercises strengthen their "chops", but they will also help them to play these styles with more musical flair. In addition, there are accompaniment tracks featuring professional musicians playing in those styles.

How to Use This Book and Play-along Tracks

This book is generally organized from easiest to hardest workouts. Yes, it is an exercise book, but there are many forms of exercise. Please master each chapter before proceeding to the next one. When there are difficult passages, please slow down the tempo, play one hand at a time, and tap out rhythms before playing at the suggested tempo.

Many (not all) workouts have a corresponding play-along track. There will always be a two measure count-off before the first measure of the workout.

INTRODUCTION

Hand Position

In my teaching experience, I have found that hand position problems occur when one of two things happen. Either the hand is overly flat or the hand is overly arched (claw). In reality, a balanced, curved, and relaxed position will work best most of the time.

A True Story...

Back when I was still in my twenties, I had the good fortune to meet professional baseball pitcher Tom Seaver when I was playing in a jazz club. I had an interest in pitching for baseball and he had an interest in jazz piano. I inquired about the technique in throwing a slider. He replied, "Well, show me how to play [the piano] like that and I'll show you." I responded, "Pretend you have a baseball in each hand. Turn your hands over and you will have good hand position [for playing the piano]." He then gave me a nice tip on how to throw that elusive pitch.

Here are some things to keep in mind regarding this technique:
- Turn both palms up.
- Put a baseball (or softball for larger hands) in each hand.
- Take care to not grip the baseball.
- Treat it more like an egg.
- Turn palms down and let baseballs drop.
- Place your hands over the piano keys.

Warm-Up and Stretching Exercises

Ways to warm up cold hands:
- Rub hands together.
- Shake hands and fingers.
- Use one hand to massage the other.
- Put palms together and expand all fingers in a comfortable stretch.
- Close fist, then open.

INTRODUCTION

Stretching exercises: Start by planting the thumb and stretching the other fingers.

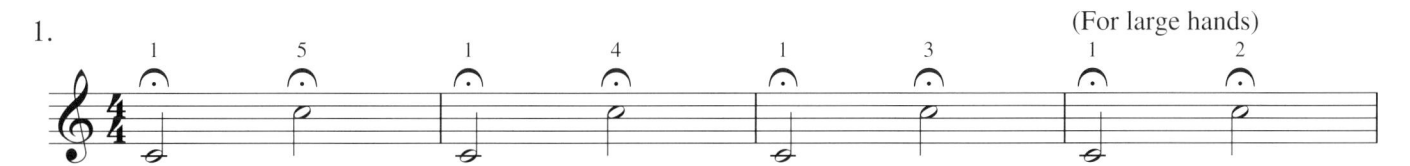

1.

Now, stretch the left hand.

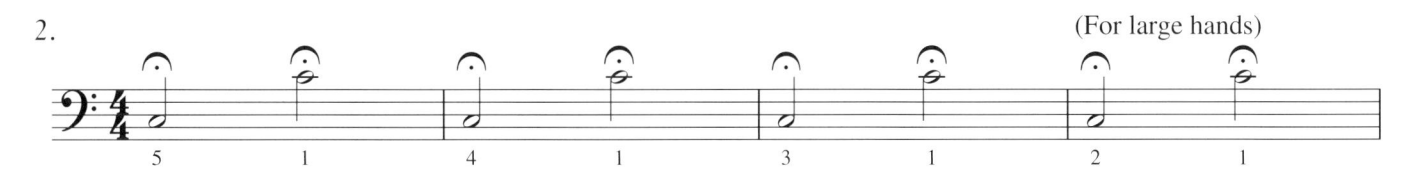

2.

If your hand is larger you can try a larger interval. Here are some other stretches.
Please follow the fingerings and take your time.

3.

4.

5. **Play slowly**

3

PIANO AEROBICS

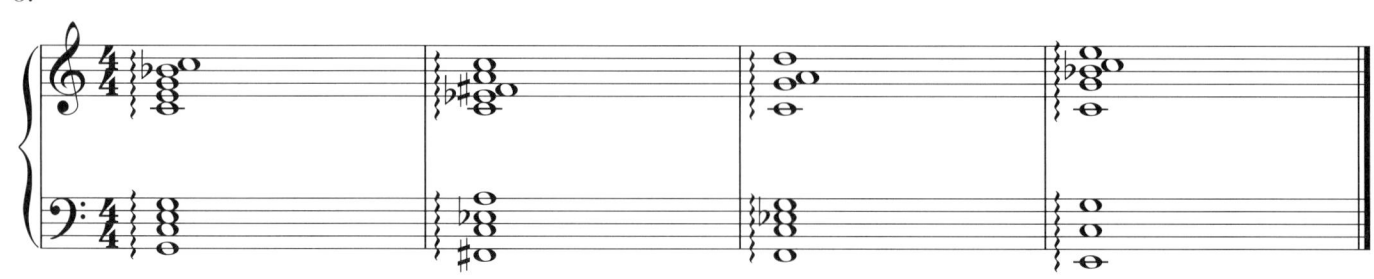

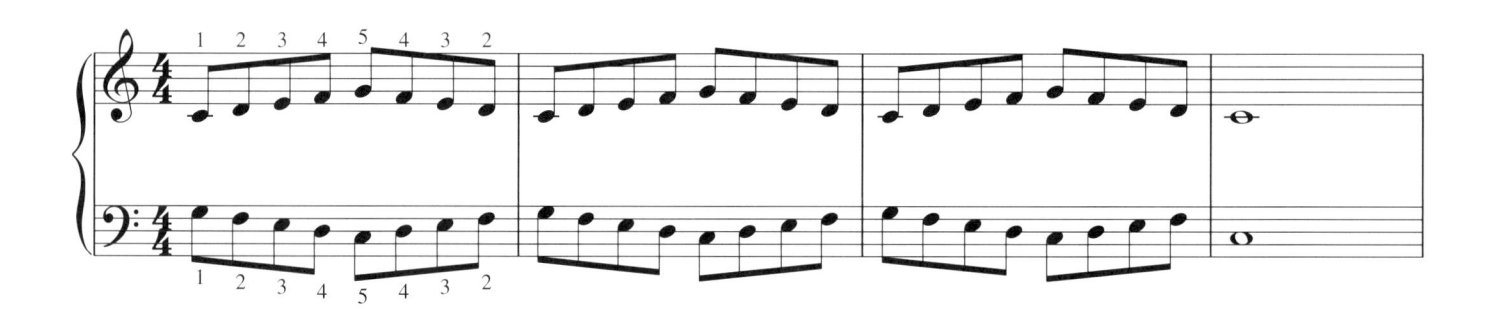

6.

7.

WEEKS 1-2

KEEPING TIME WHILE BUILDING STRENGTH

The Metronome: Make It Your Trusted Friend

- It is a great tool that can help smooth out technique.
- It trains the musician to keep a constant tempo.
- It is essential for modern styles of music, such as those found in this book.

To play with a metronome:

- Set your metronome to quarter note = 60.
- Turn on the metronome.
- Tap or clap the following figures matching the quarter note pulse.

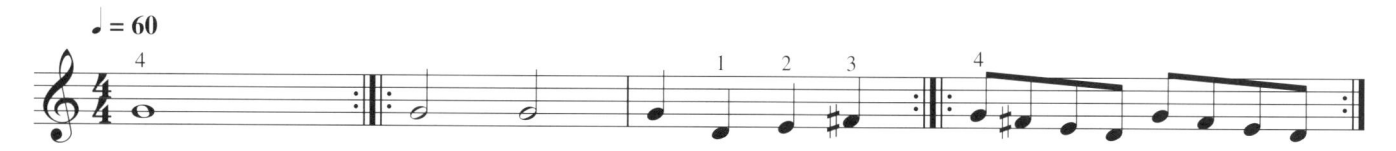

Mastery of the metronome takes practice!

If you are having trouble playing in time, here are some possible suggestions:

- Clap or tap the rhythms.
- It is important to listen carefully and play exactly with the click. In general, if you are in sync, you will hear the click less.
- Relax. It will take awhile to internalize the click and listen.

Musicians refer to keeping good time as a "groove". The term "groove" also refers to the spot where an old phonograph record needle sits while playing a record.

Finger Strengthening Exercise

These exercises will start with the three strongest fingers. Play each of these several times before proceeding to the next one. In order to get the most from this and most other finger exercise, please lift all fingers high. Pay special attention to the weaker 4th and 5th fingers.

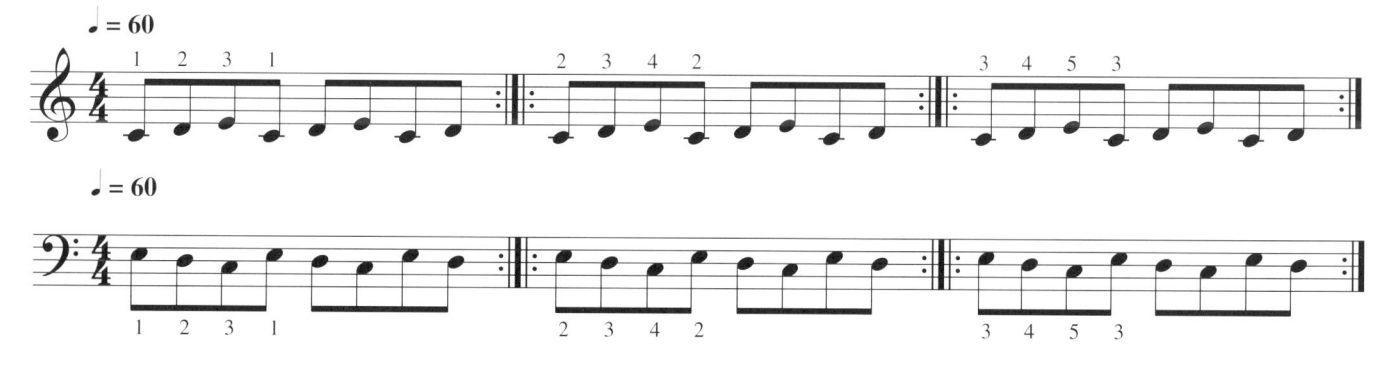

Finger Strengthening Workout #1

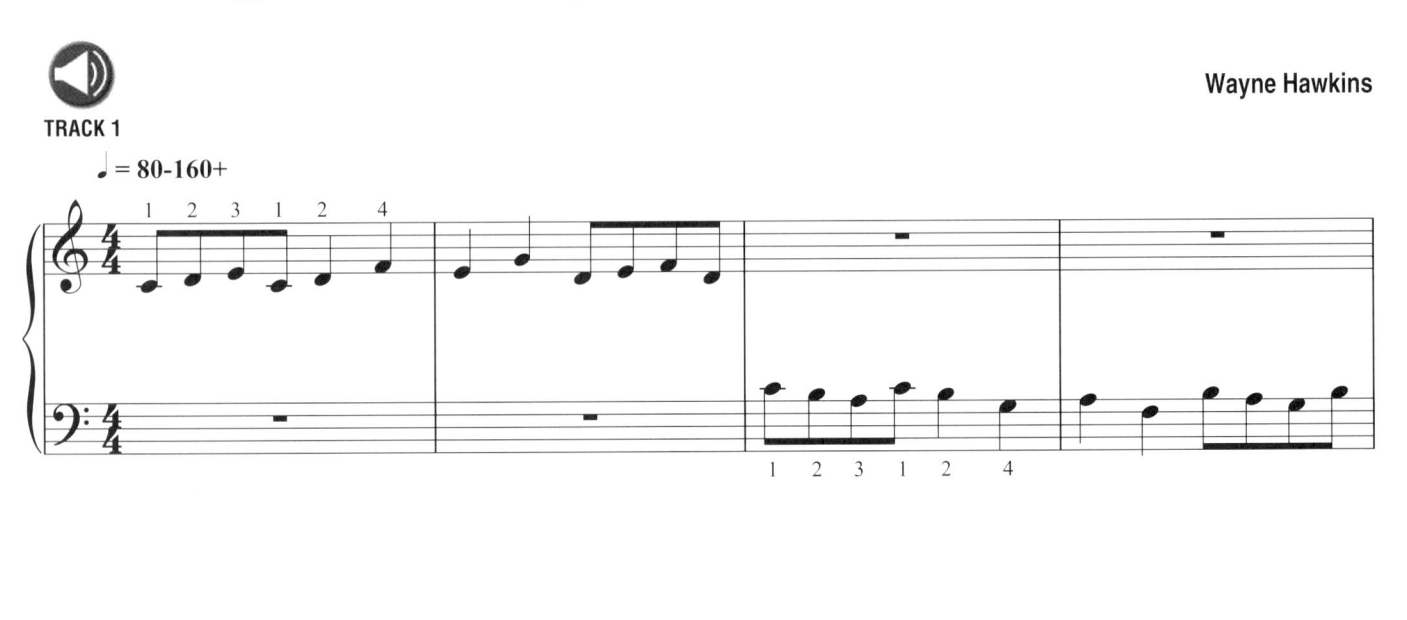

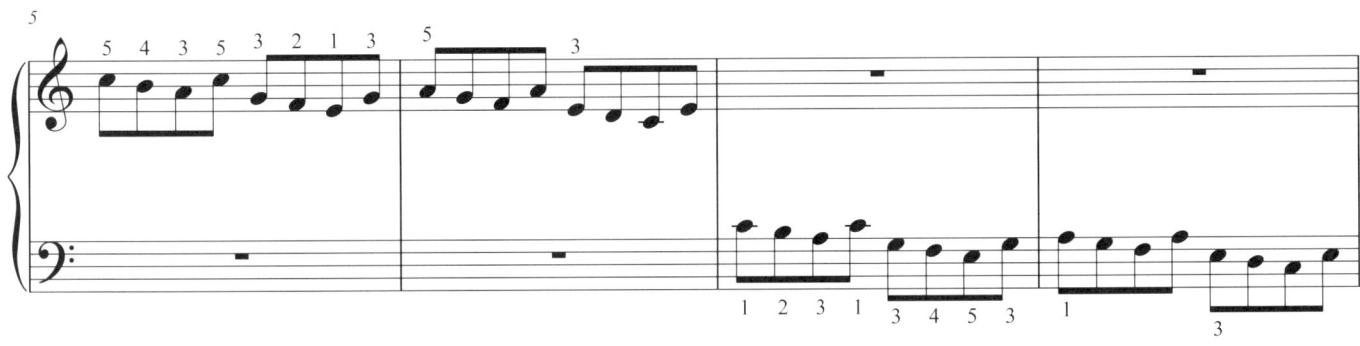

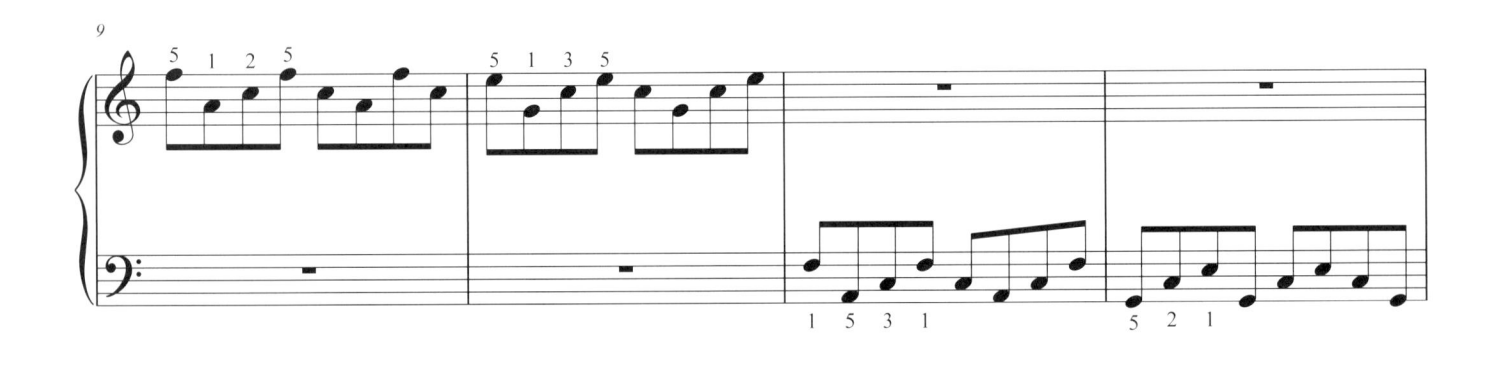

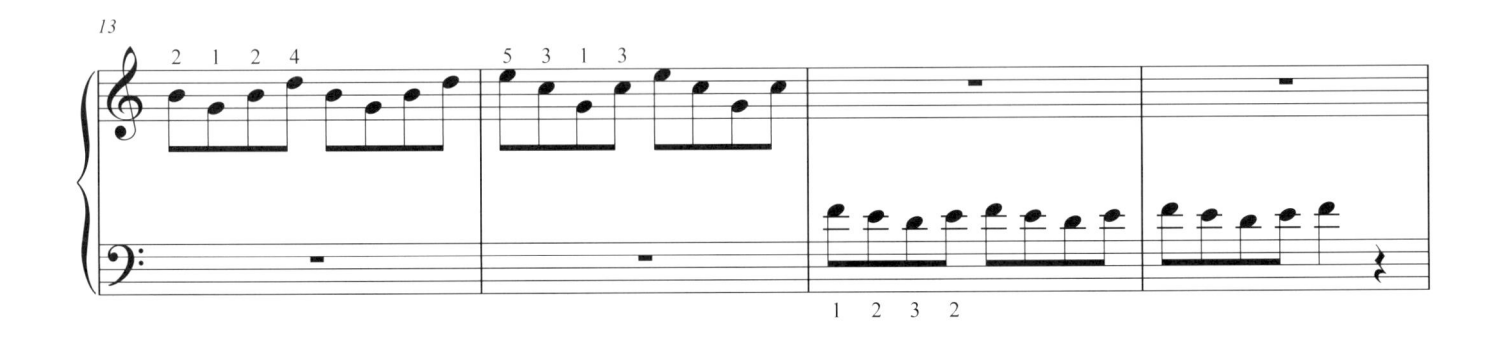

Wayne Hawkins

TRACK 1

♩ = 80-160+

17
21
25
29
33

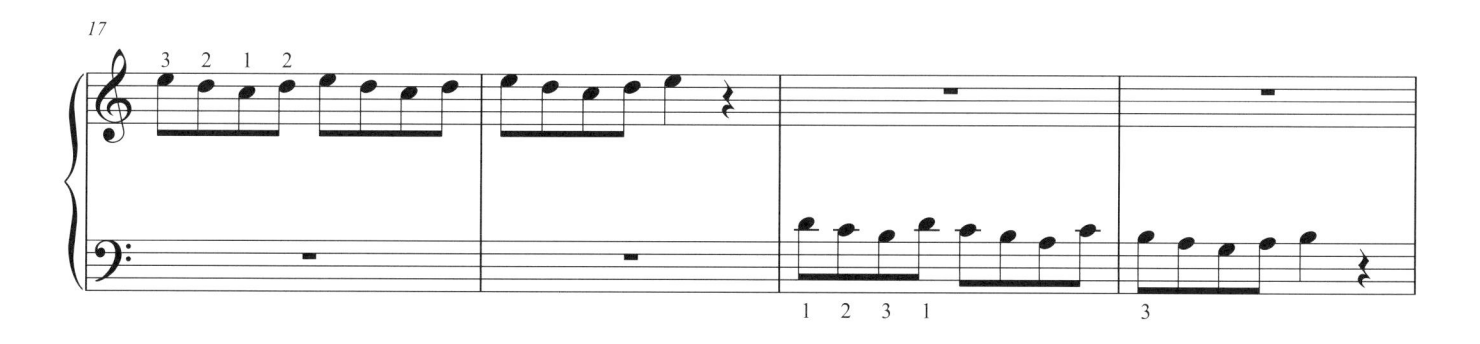

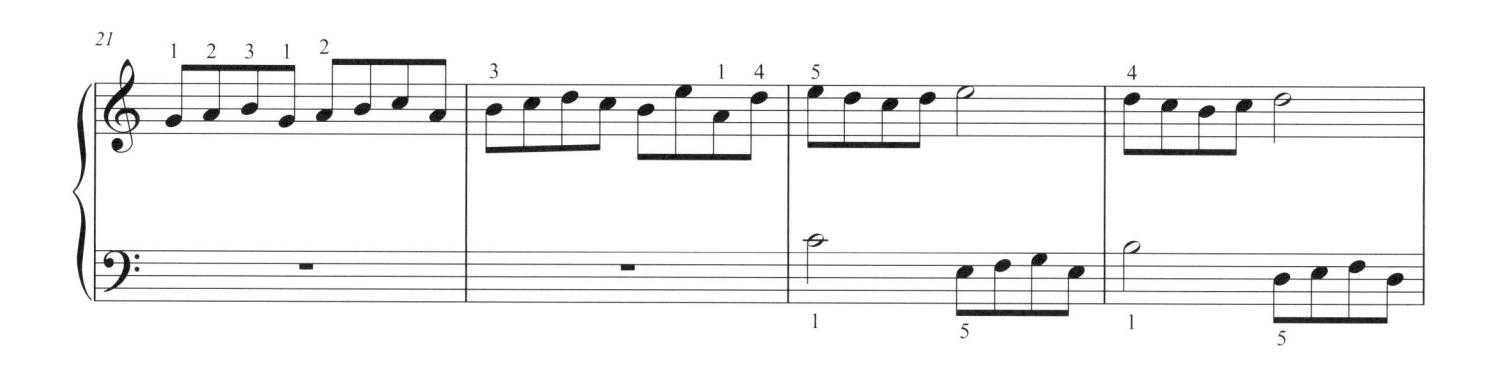

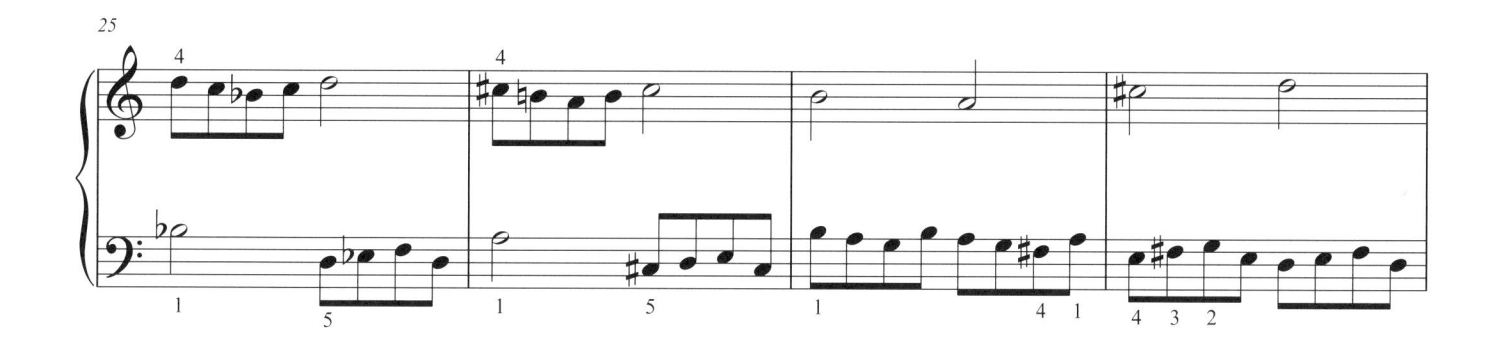

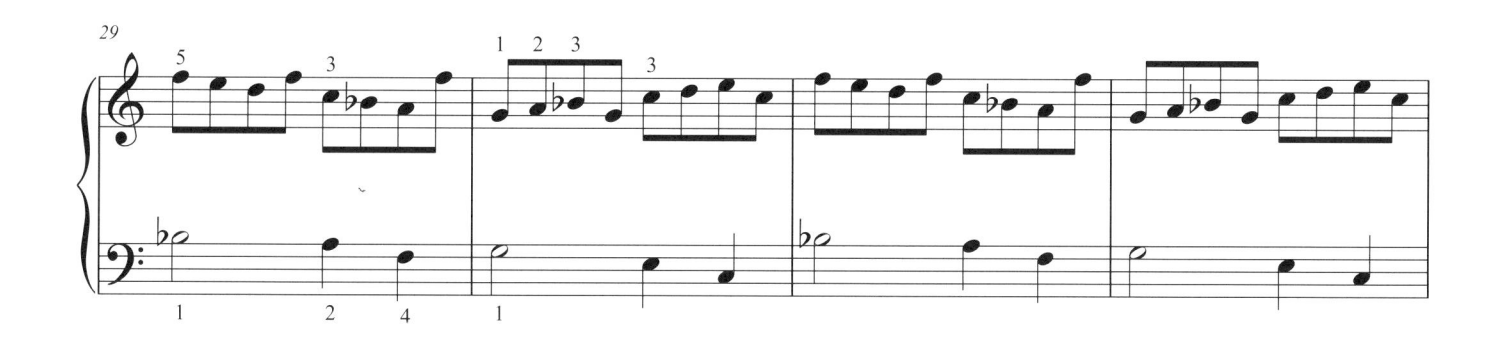

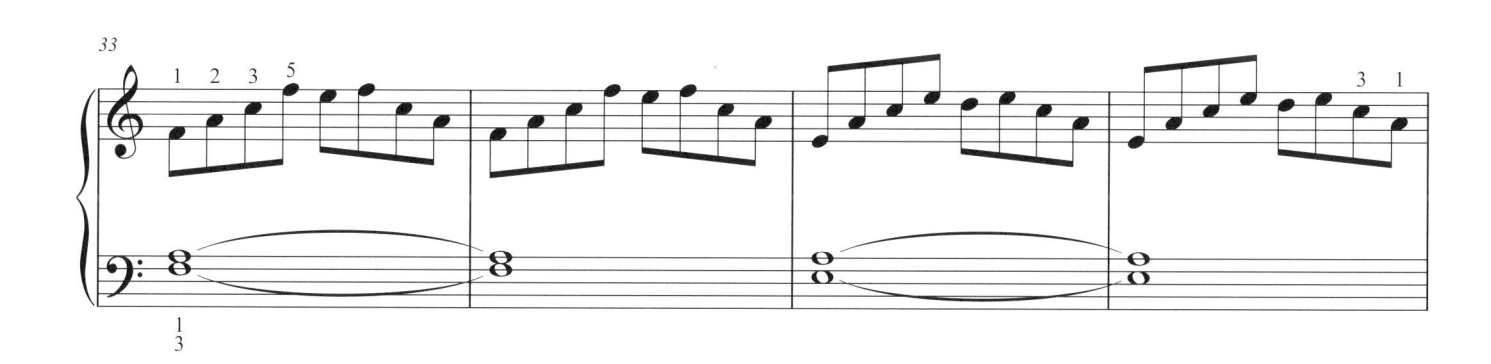

PIANO AEROBICS

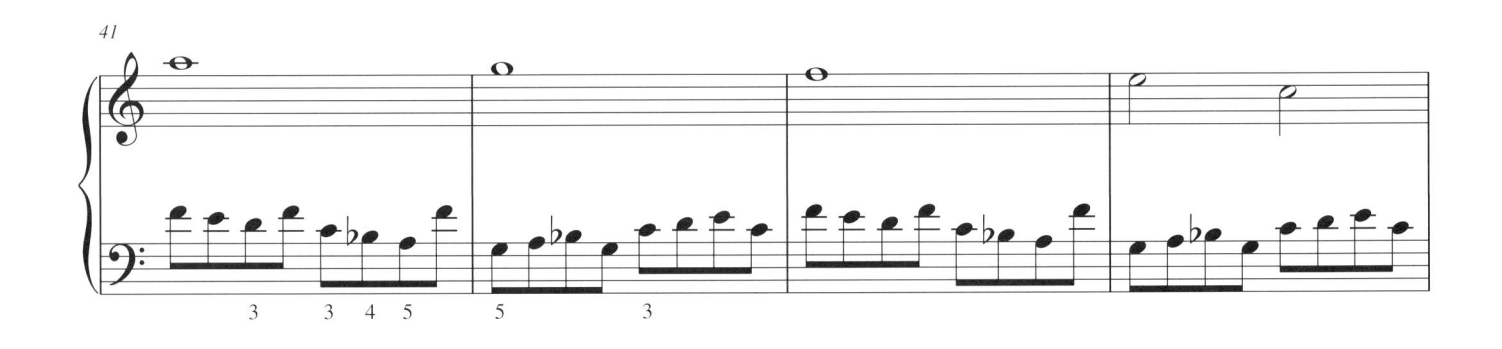

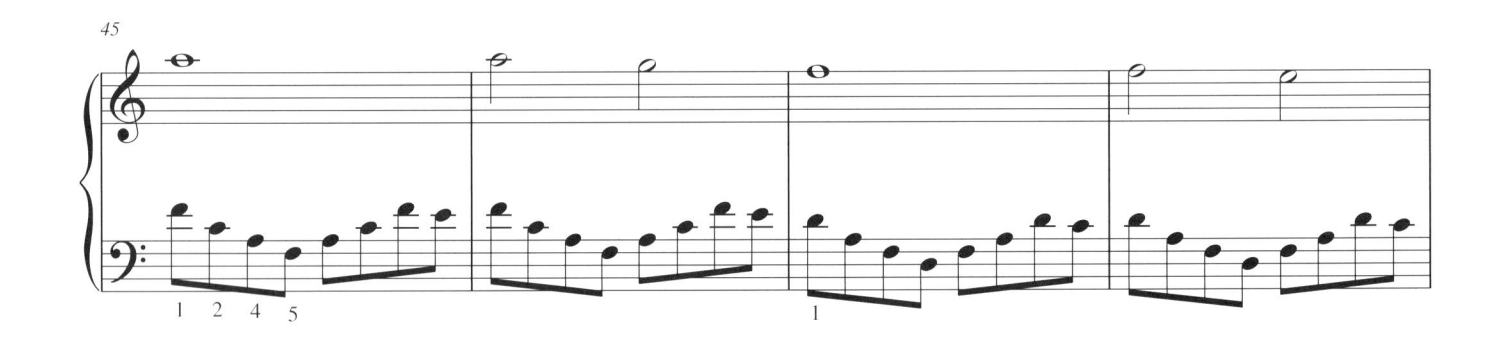

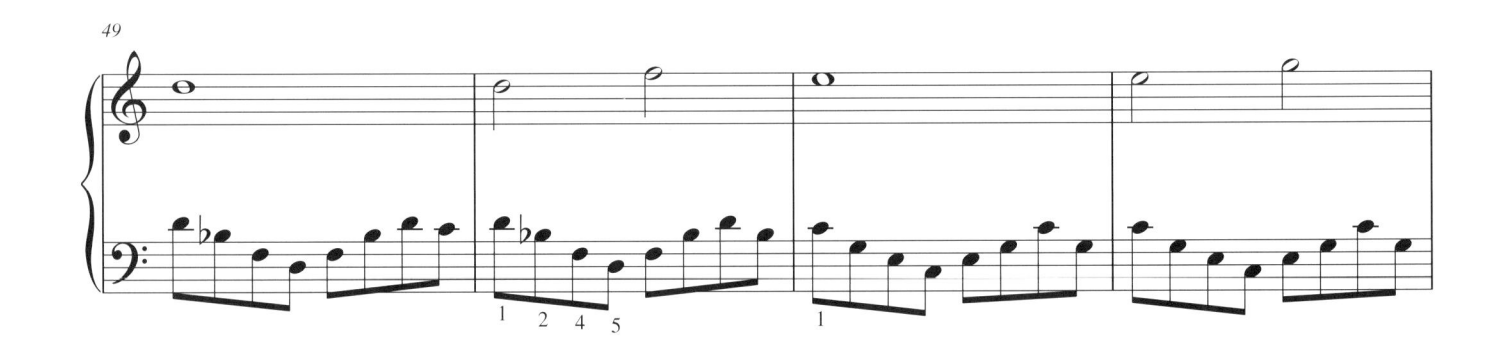

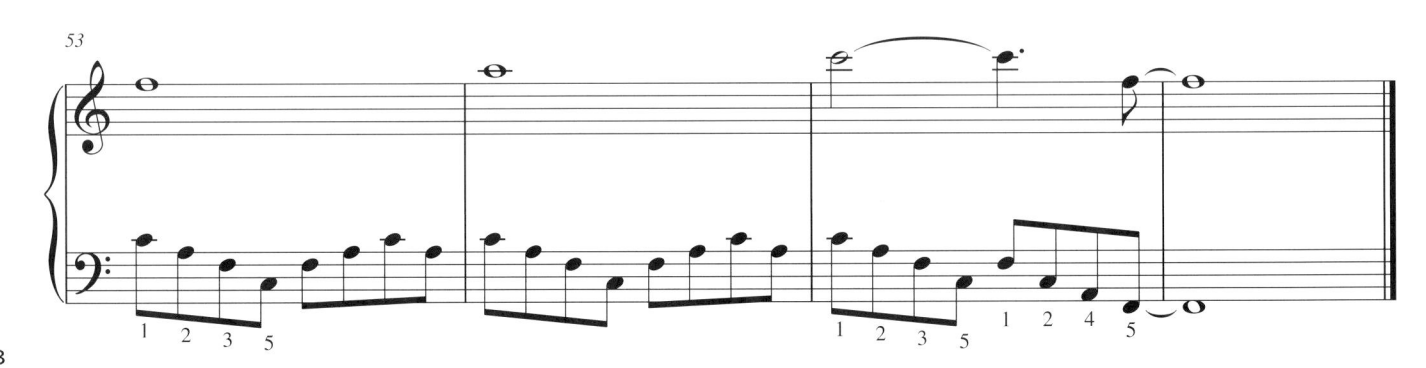

WEEKS 3-4

WORKING WITH THE LEFT HAND

How to Swing Eighth Notes

Ostinato

Below is a typical ostinato bass line found in boogie woogie. The quarter notes remain steady. Play the bass line to understand the basic form.

What is Swing?

Classically trained musicians often have an initial problem with swing style. The essence of swing, shuffle and boogie woogie is found in the eighth note sub-division. Eighth notes in these styles should not be even.

Below are three different counting schemes to play swing. Play each figure as written. Ultimately, you want to be able to play straight eighth notes with a swing triplet subdivision.

a) First, the figure is written as a dotted eighth-sixteenth. Note that if the dotted figure is counted accurately, the result is a jerky swing feel.

b) Now the first eighth note is counted as two thirds of a triplet with the second eighth note on the last third. This is actually closer to a swing feel.

c) Below is an even eighth note ostinato. Play this figure with the rhythmic feel of example b. If you still have trouble, try saying the words BOOgie WOOgie, to feel the rhythm of the eighth notes.

PIANO AEROBICS

Left Hand Development

Play the figure below as indicated by the fingering. Practice smooth execution and ease in your playing. At first, most pianists have trouble playing octaves in this fashion. Instead of reaching for the octave each time, keep your hand open the distance of an octave.

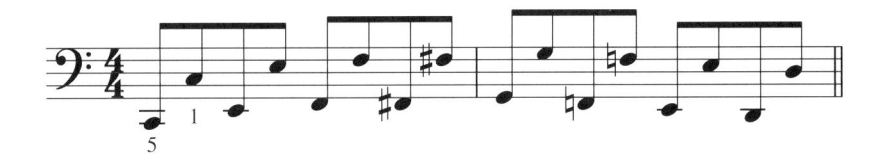

Play this figure as indicated by the fingering. Play with a metronome and practice clean execution. Gradually increase the tempo to ♩ = 108.

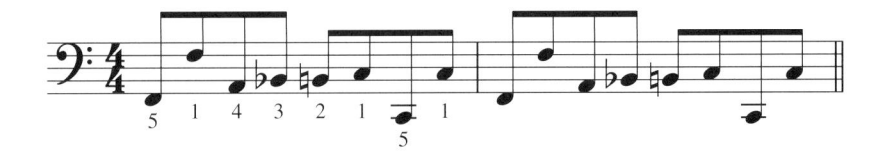

After you have completed these exercises, proceed to the workout. Time to have fun!

BOOGIE WOOGIE WORKOUT

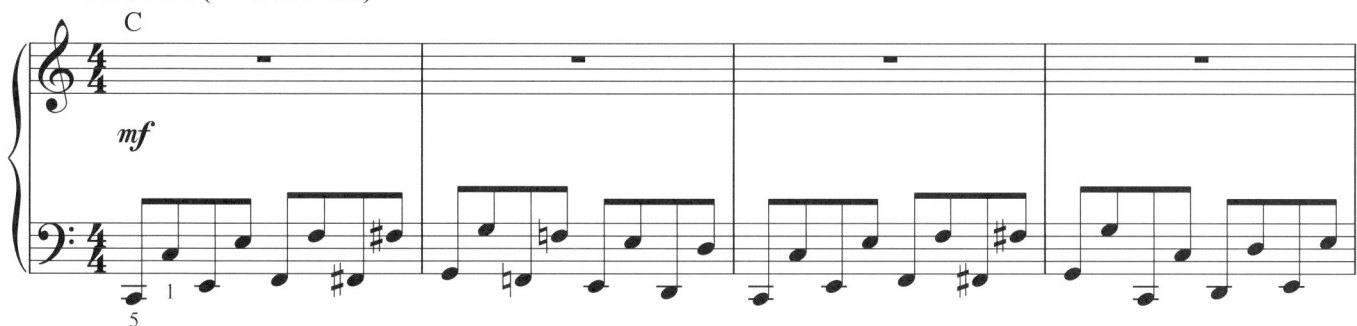

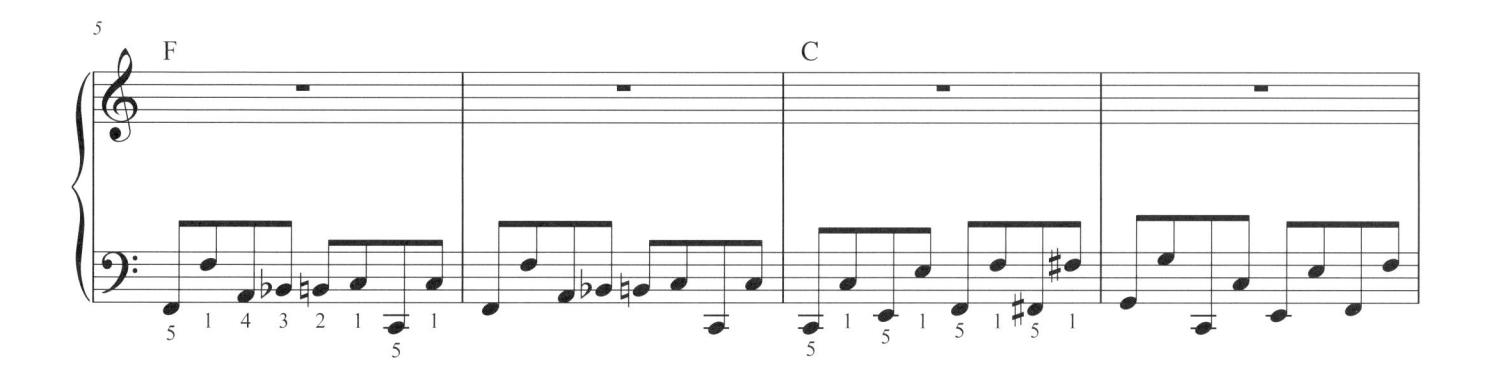

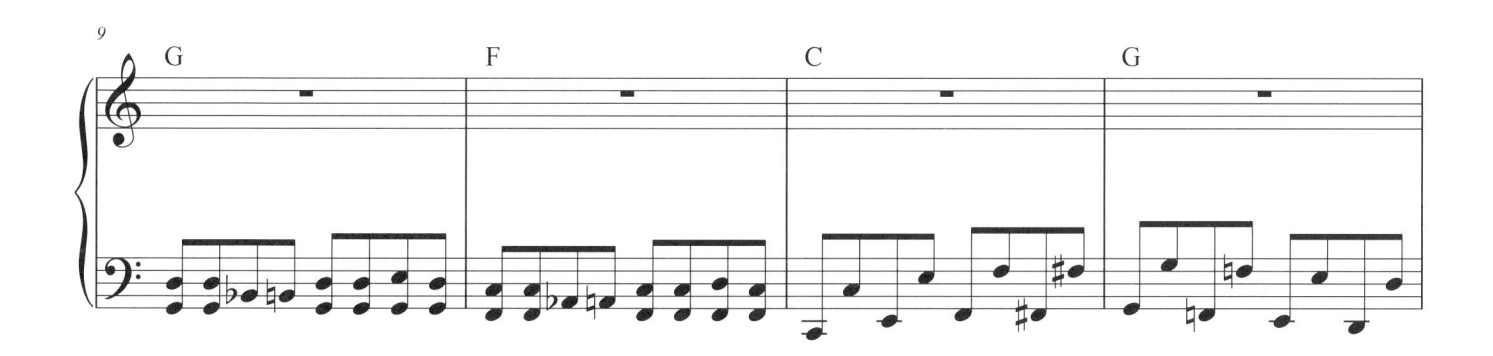

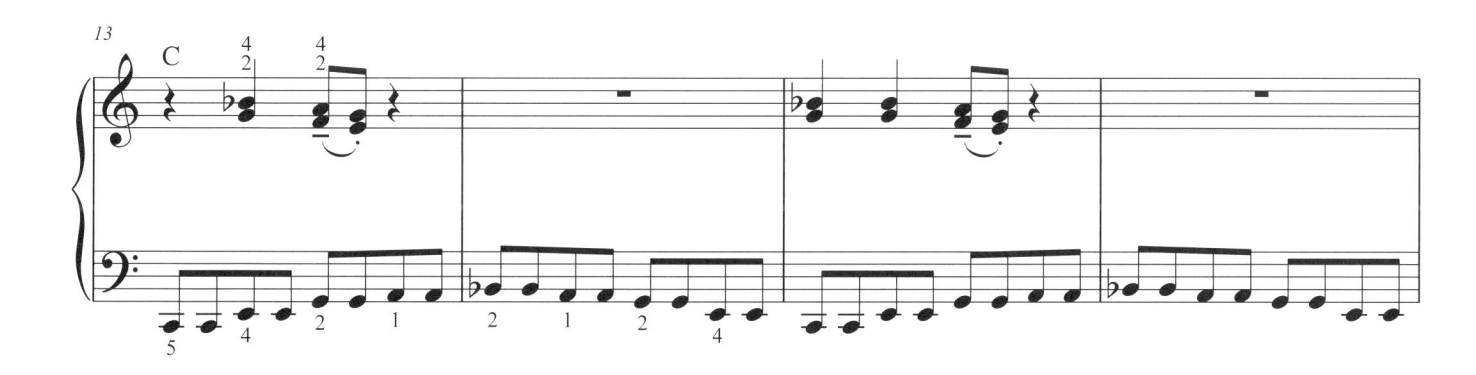

Wayne Hawkins

Moderato (♩ = c. 108-130)

PIANO AEROBICS

WEEKS 5-6
PLAYING INDEPENDENTLY

Hand Independence, Working with Ostinato

Play the figure below:

Observe that every note played is on a strong beat except for the last note of the second measure. If this is difficult to play accurately, try tapping the rhythms out on the lid of the piano. To assure accuracy, try tapping eighth notes in your right hand, and the ostinato pattern in your left hand. This method of using a subdivision to ensure accurate counting will solve most potential rhythm problems in this section.

Please note the following measure that needs special attention. Using the half note as the strong beat, start by tapping the right-hand rhythm of the measure below. In this measure, the subdivision of the half note is three even quarter notes. Try tapping half notes in your left hand and quarter note triplets in your right.
With careful practice, both figures will fit together.

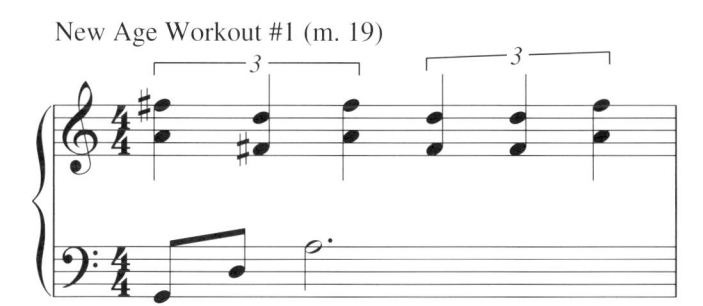

New Age Workout #1 (m. 19)

How to Use the Damper (Sustain) Pedal

The sustain (or damper) pedal is a great tool of expression. It is, however, a very sensitive part of the piano and is often misunderstood. Some piano literature includes precise pedal markings. Most contemporary lead sheets and piano arrangements will leave pedaling to your discretion. One technical point that was made to me years ago (by a veteran of many a recording session) was to be as quiet as possible when using the sustain pedal. In other words, avoid the thud! Do not let the full weight of your foot rest on the pedal. Overuse of the damper pedal presents another problem by blurring a phrase that should be clear.

When playing scale-like passages at slower tempos, using the pedal carefully can enhance the singing quality of a passage without sacrificing clarity. In this situation, it is best to lightly pedal each note.

Other general pedaling choices include:

Simply refreshing the pedal with each new phrase.

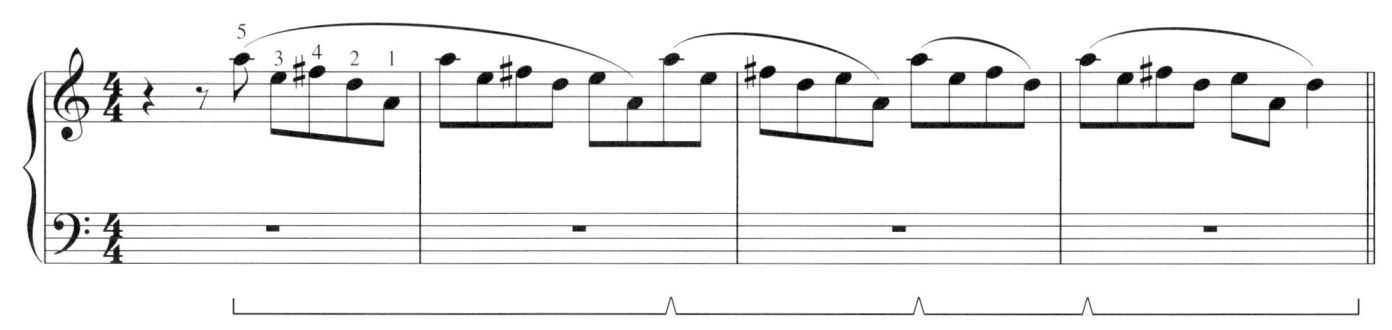

Refresh the pedal with every change in harmony.

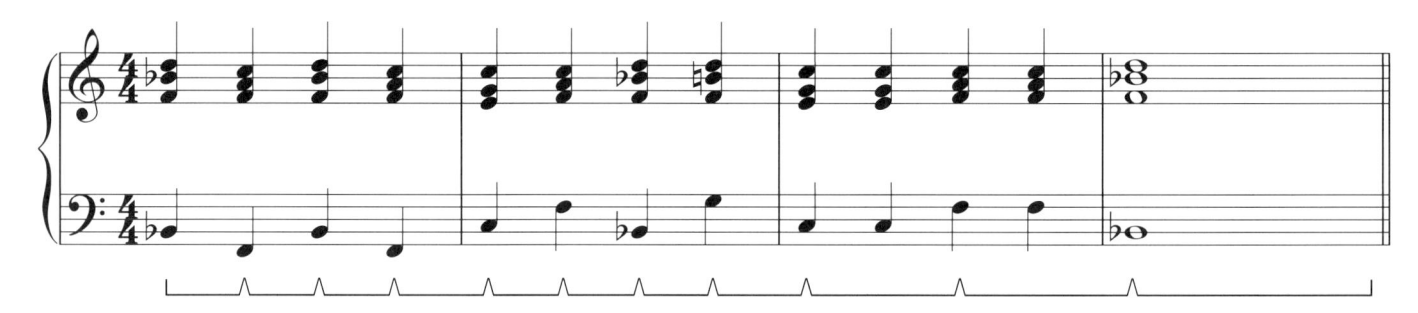

Refresh pedal based on style and changes in harmony.

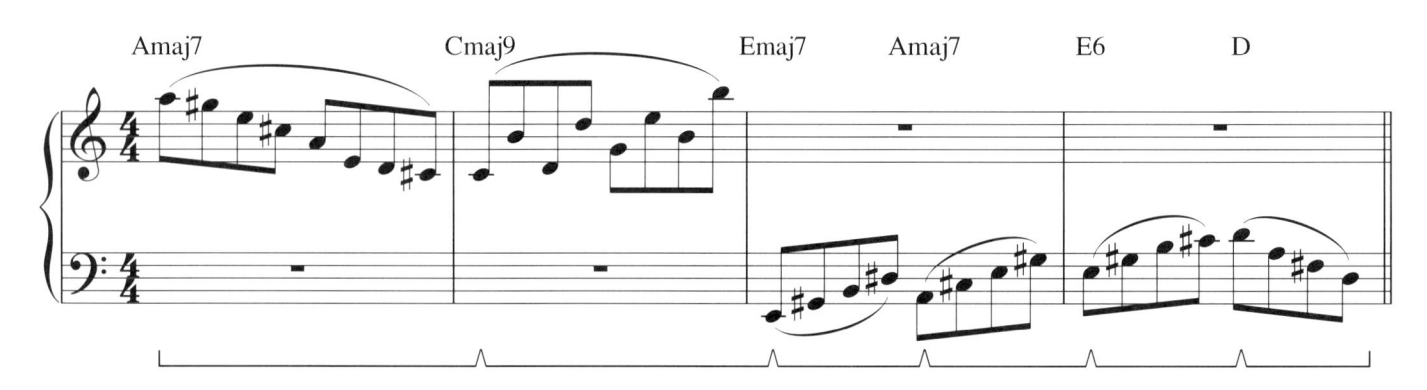

It is important not to pedal through rests.

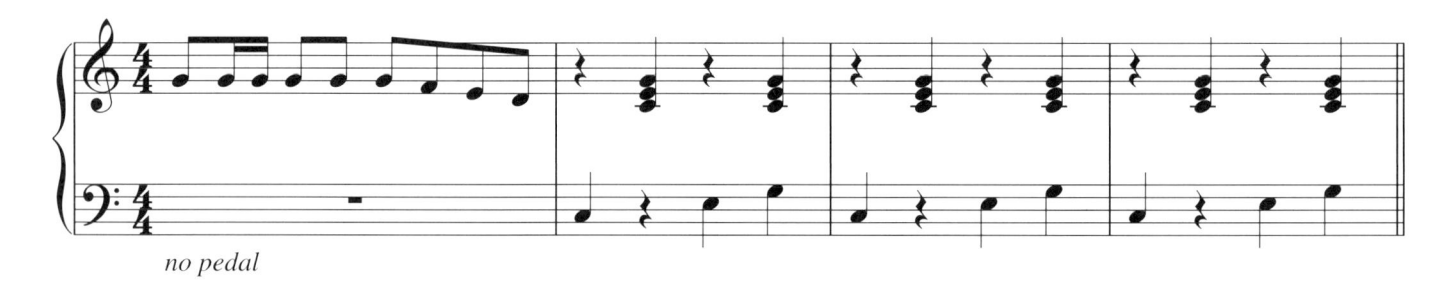

no pedal

NEW AGE WORKOUT #1

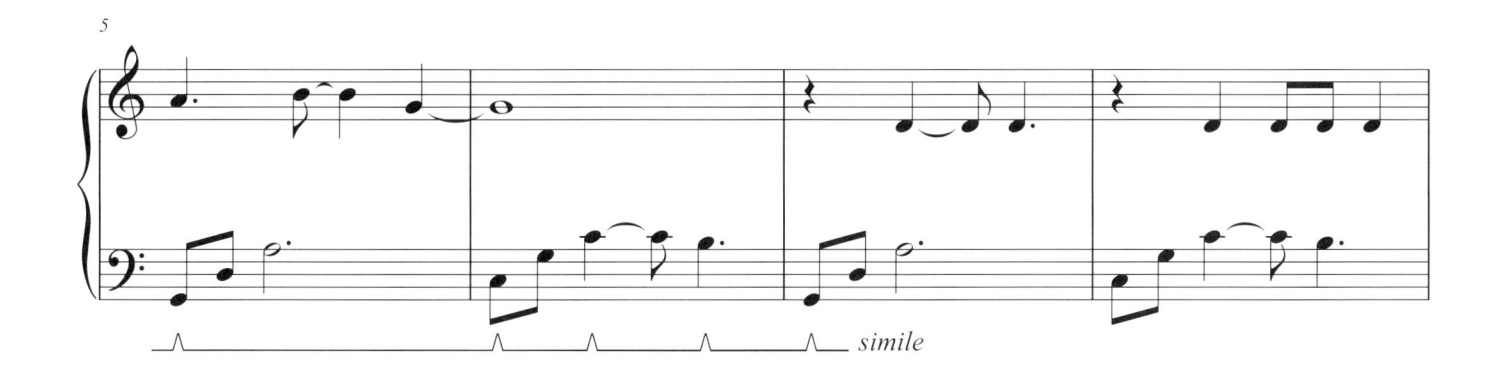

Wayne Hawkins

PIANO AEROBICS

WEEKS 5-6

WEEKS 7-8
ARTICULATIONS

Interpreting Articulations

Now that we are on the road to a richer overall sound, let's turn our attention to the different ways that notes can speak.

A **slur** is used to connect notes with no space between them.

Staccatos create short, detached notes. Generally a quarter note will get an eighth note value.

Tenuto (literally means "hold") is held for the full note value.

An **accent** on a note means greater emphasis. In other words when struck, the note is more dynamic.

Articulation Exercises

These exercises combine the different articulations.

1. Observe the slur and connect the first two notes and then contrast the last two notes with staccato.

2. Play this slur-staccato pattern combined with tenuto.

3. Play the exercise below that adds an accent to the other articulations.

ARTICULATION WORKOUT

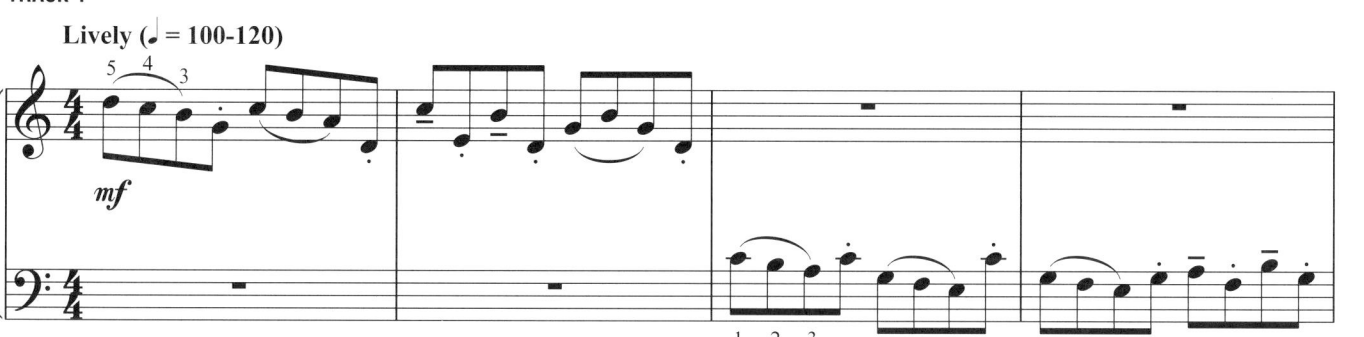

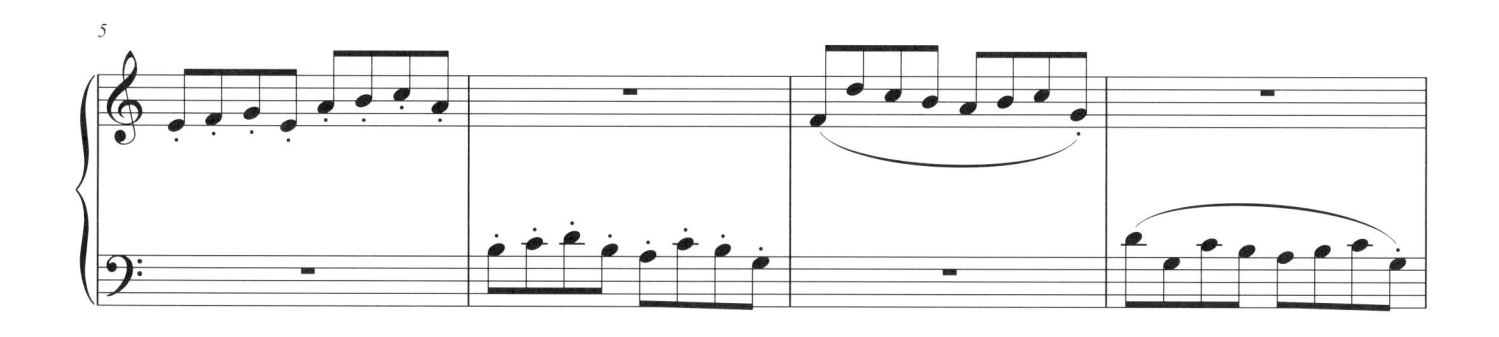

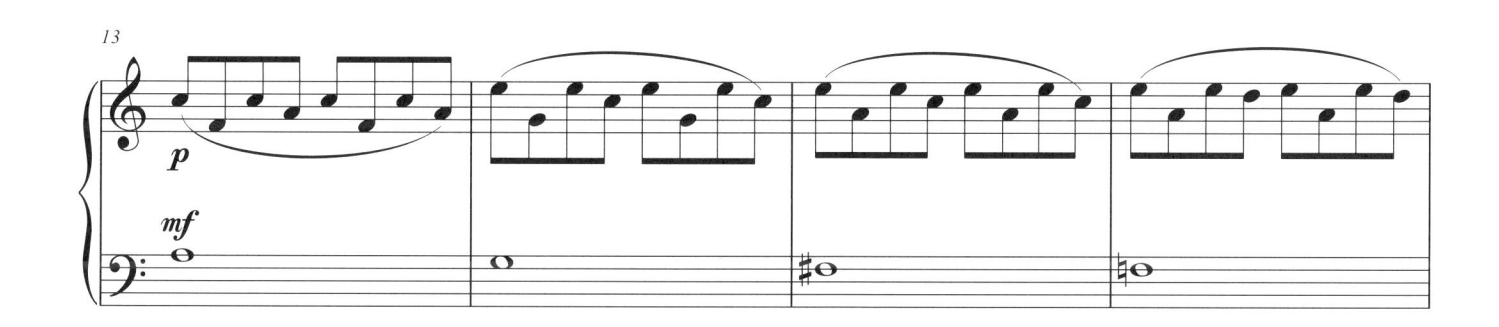

Wayne Hawkins

17
f
2 3 1 5
21
p
mf
25
29
34
mp

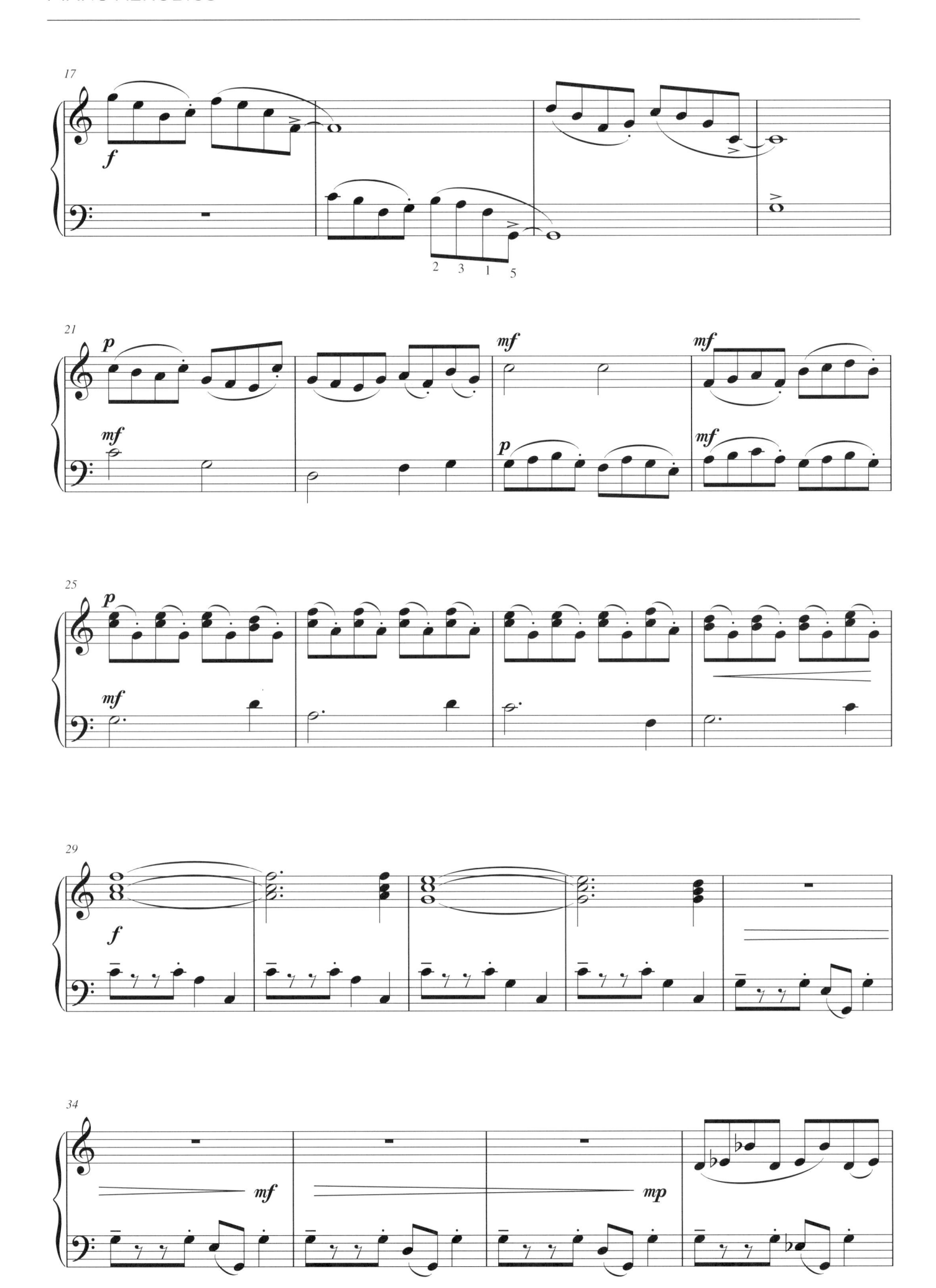

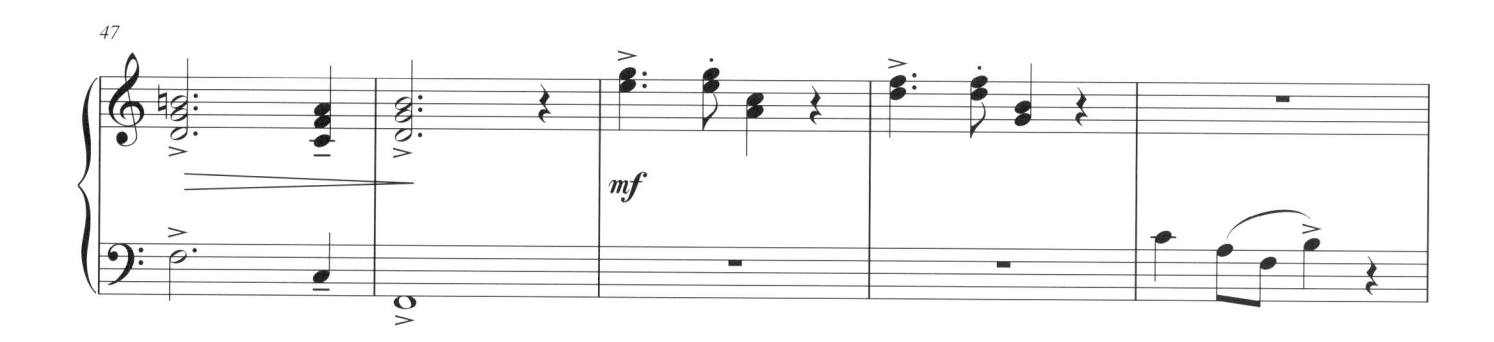

WEEKS 7–8

WEEKS 9-10
PLAYING ROCK PIANO

Wrist Articulations

This section prepares the pianist for repetitive tasks such as heavy chord playing. To perform such wrist articulations, position the right hand over the keys. Play using your thumb and fifth finger on each note as indicated below:

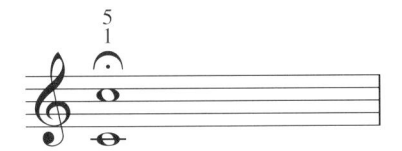

Now, pick your hand up by only bending your wrist and play with a relaxed wrist.

Wrist Exercises

To play this exercise correctly, fingers and forearms should remain relatively still. When playing octaves, bend your wrist (not the arm) to move fingers up and down.

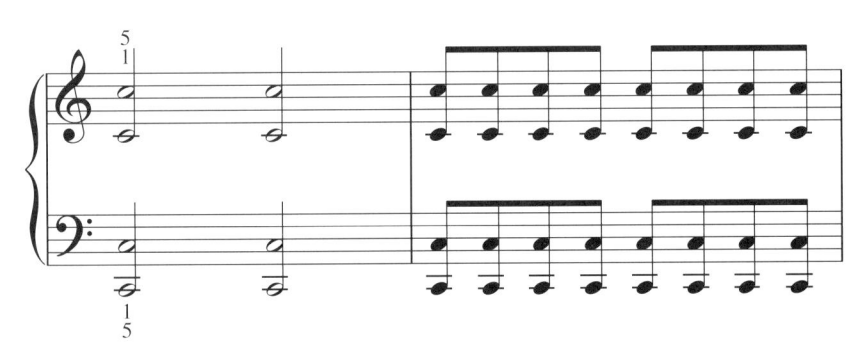

Observation

There are several things to observe while performing these initial exercises:
- Is the wrist moving without the help of the forearm?
- Are the arms and shoulders relaxed?
- Am I allowing the wrist do the work?
- Remember to relax. It should feel like you are simply waving the hand up and down.

ROCK WORKOUT

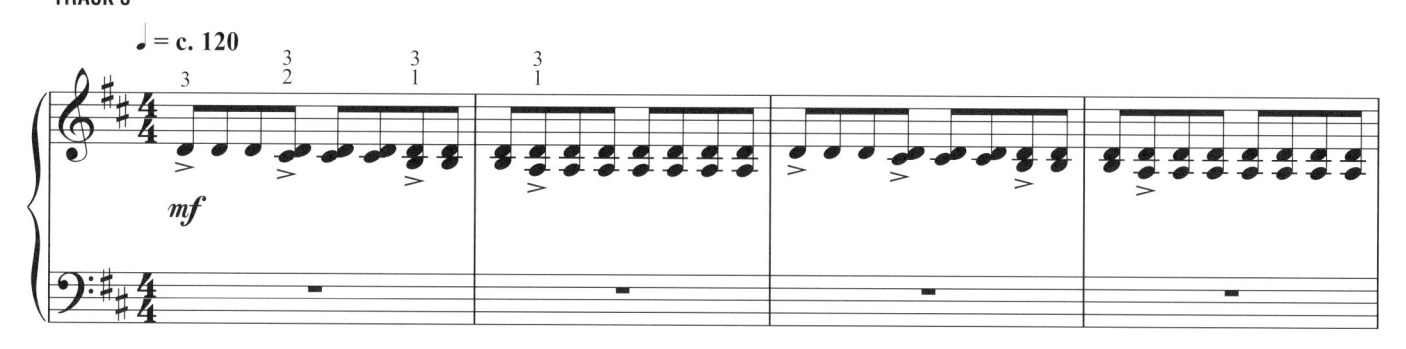

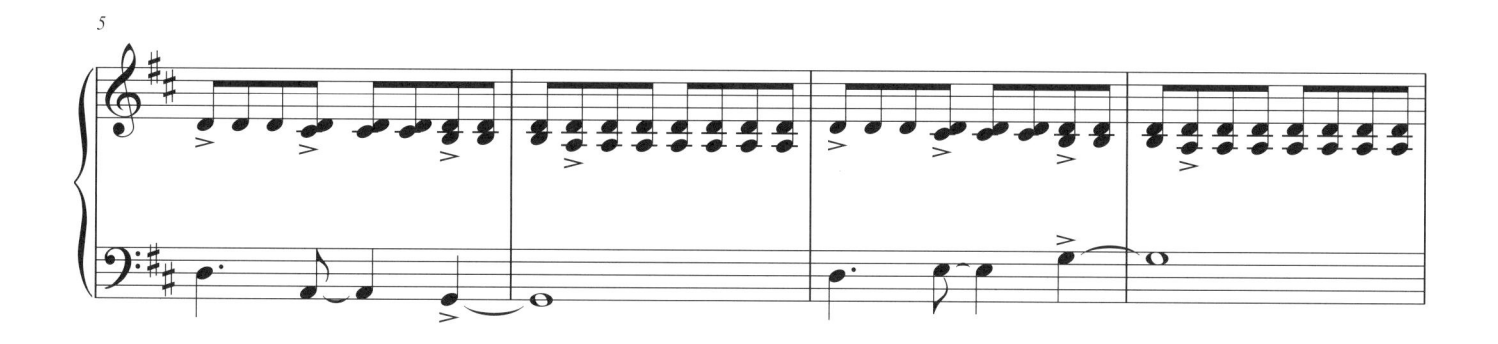

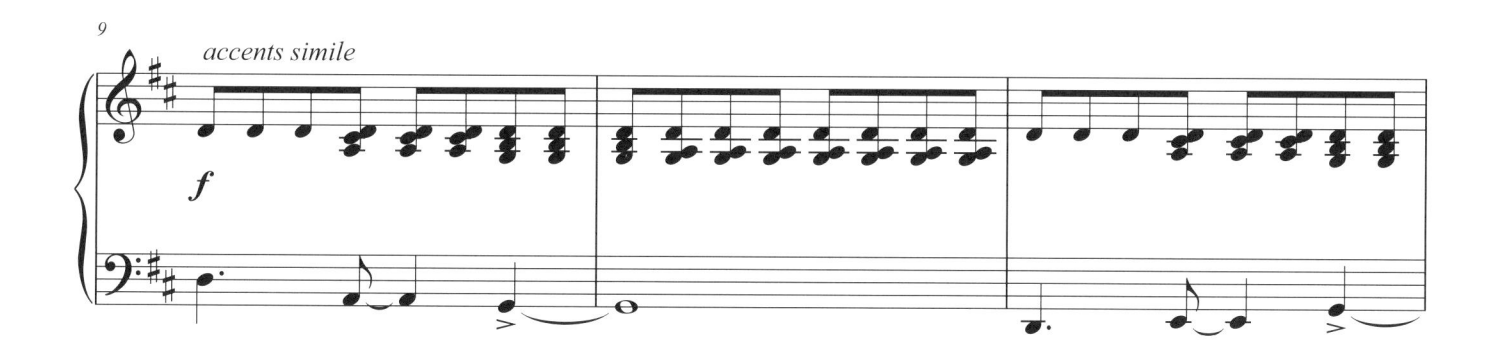

Wayne Hawkins

PIANO AEROBICS

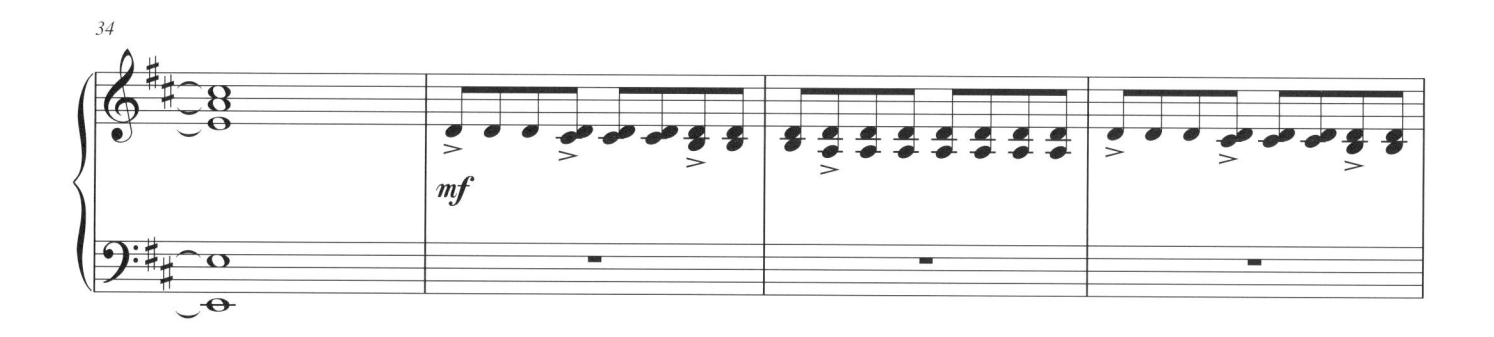

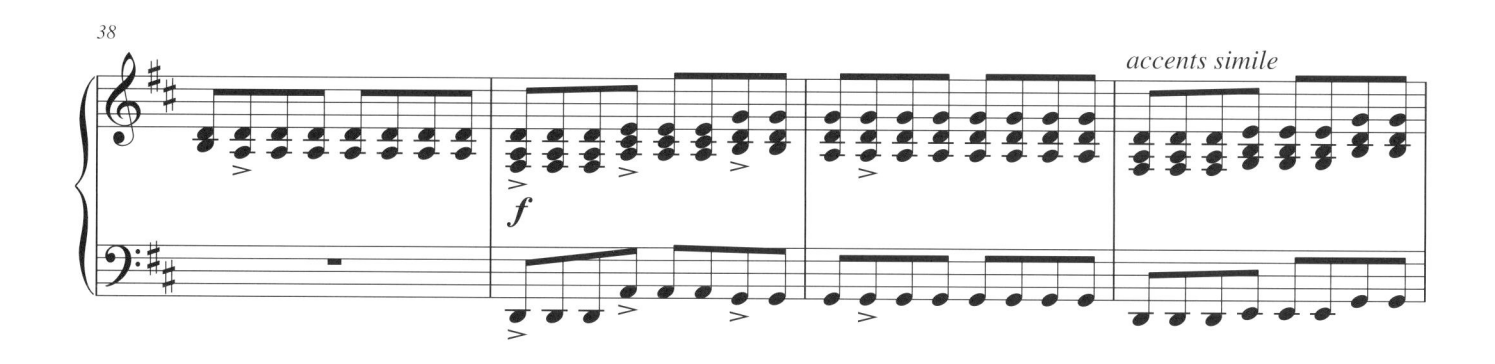

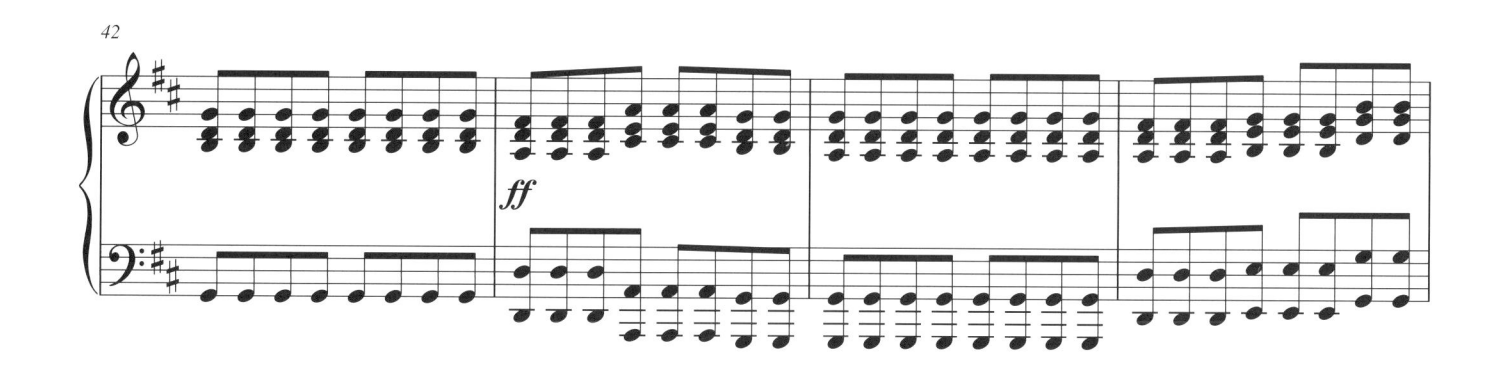

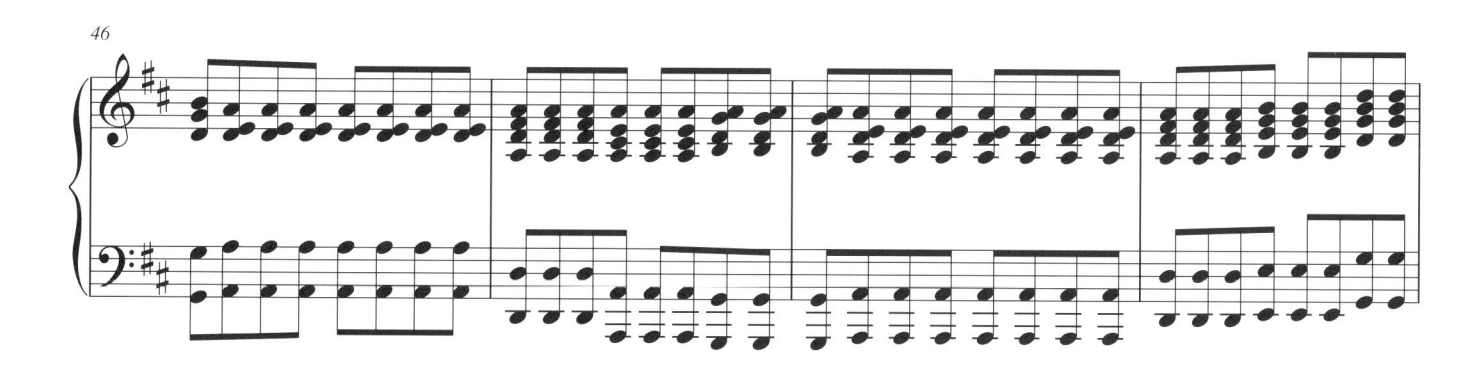

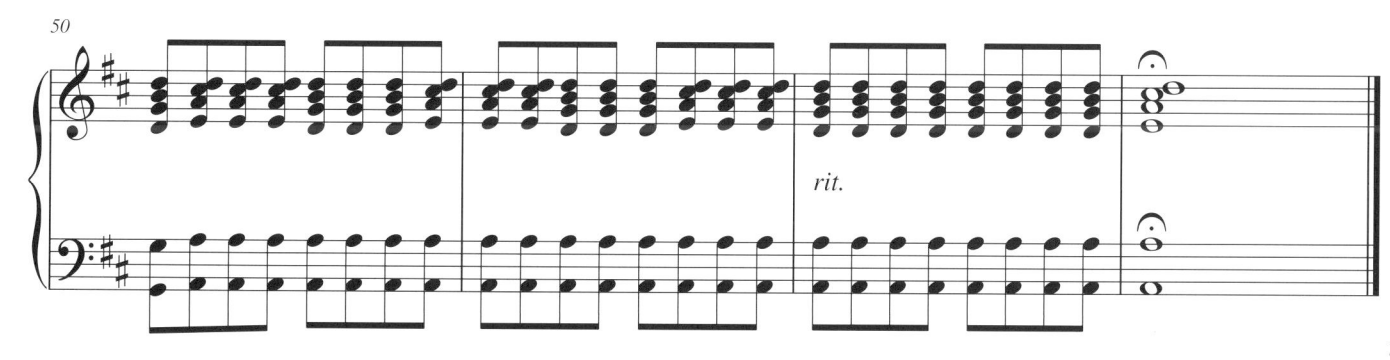

WEEKS 9–10

WEEKS 11–12

BASIC BLUES

Thinking (But Not Always Seeing) Triplets

Understanding the notation of triplets can be a challenge for a developing musician. First, look at eighth note triplets. Set your metronome to ♩ = 60. Tap the rhythm in the bar below:

1.

2. Now, play only the first and last part of the triplet.

3. As a variation, tie the first two parts of the triplets and play.

4. Swing the eighth notes below so that they sound the same as in example 3.

Blues Exercises

Pay attention to the entrance on the "and" of beat 1.

That should be coordinated the third note of the triplet.

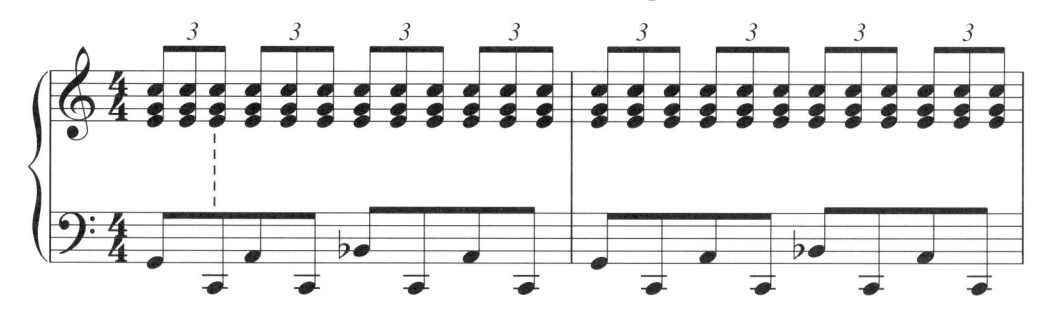

This figure has triplets and eighth notes in the right hand and eighth notes in the left hand. In this style, the first and last eighth note should be play simultaneously with the first and last part of the triplet.

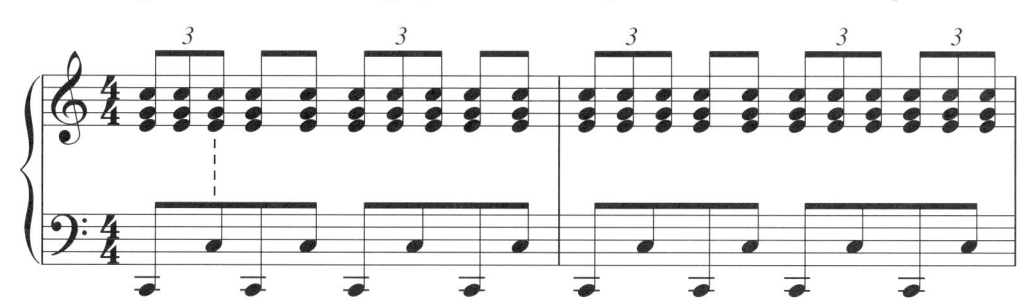

BLUES WORKOUT

Wayne Hawkins

TRACK 6

Laid-back feel (♩ = 78)

16
G7
C7
f
20
F7
C7
24
G7
F7
C7
28
decresc.
C7
mf
F7
C7
32
F7

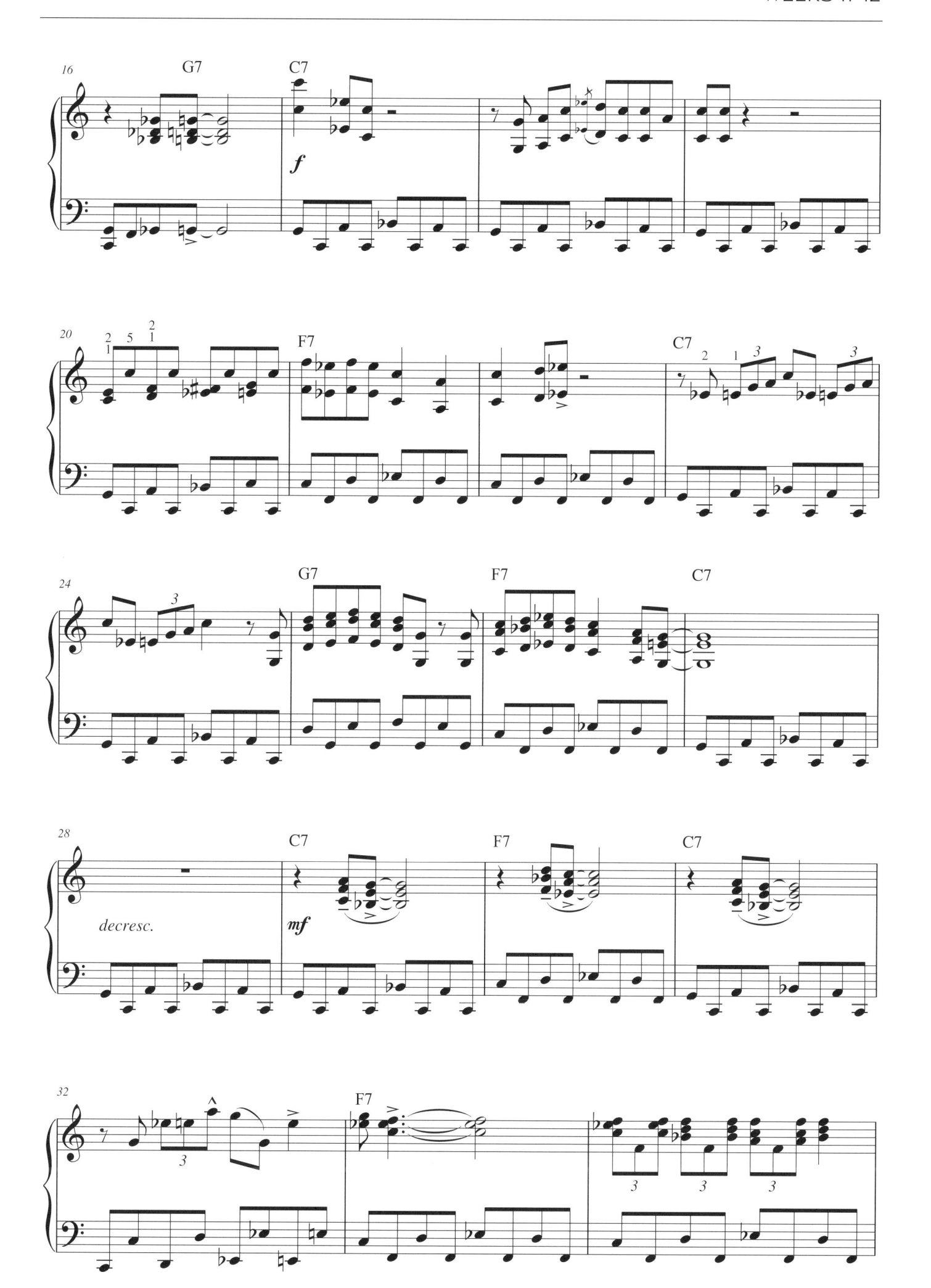

PIANO AEROBICS

WEEKS 13–14

BUILDING A BETTER TOUCH

The Importance of Touch

A pianist must be sensitive to touch in many ways. The use of arm weight is as important to legato passages as wrist playing is to staccato passages.

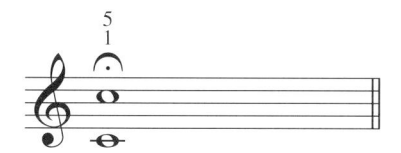

Position the right hand as indicated, then simply relax and let the hand drop onto the keys. Ideally, the majority of hand weight should rest in the fingers, while the arm and shoulder remain relaxed. For each octave, relax the arm and shoulder, then drop onto the key. This should result in a rich full tone. Please repeat until achieving proper weight distribution.

Hand and Finger Balancing

Mastering this technique will create a multi-layered sound. Start by playing this melody note with the fifth finger of the right hand.

Make sure that all the weight of the arm is in the right side of the hand. Next, it is important to over-balance when playing the figure below. In other words, the melody should always have an initial weight impulse, then a relaxed hold. For the accompaniment, finger control should help limit the dynamic level.

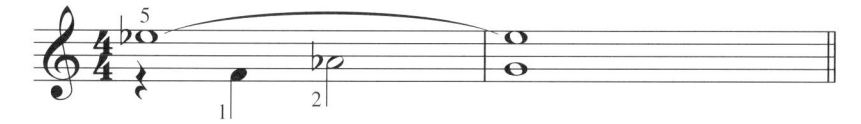

TOUCH WORKOUT

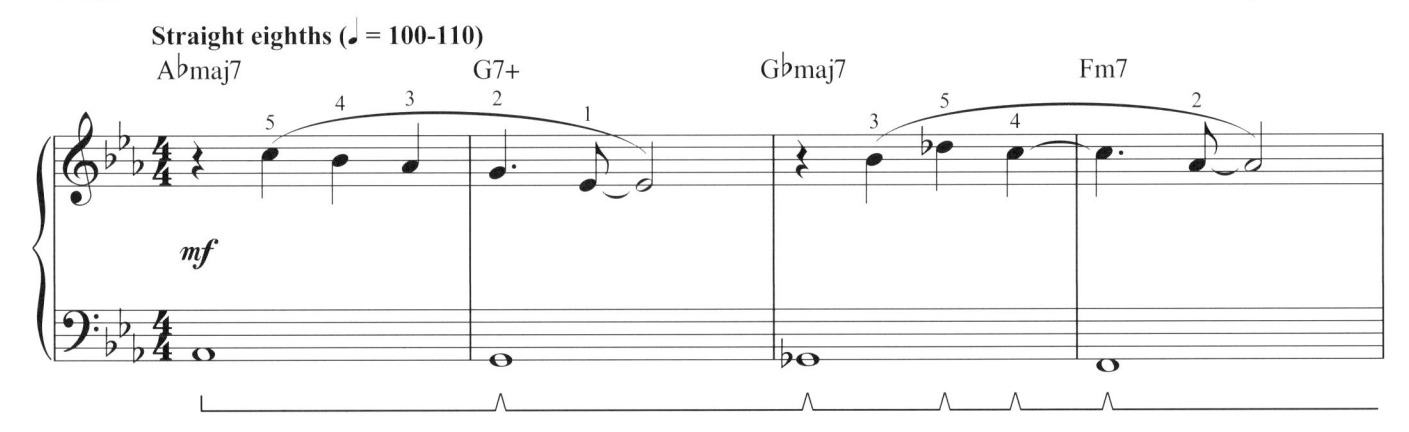

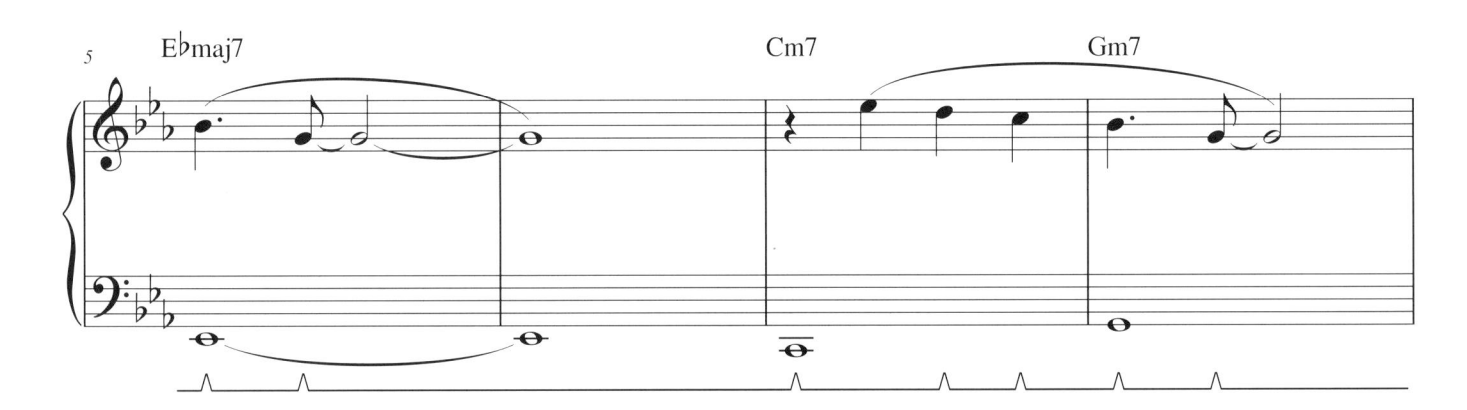

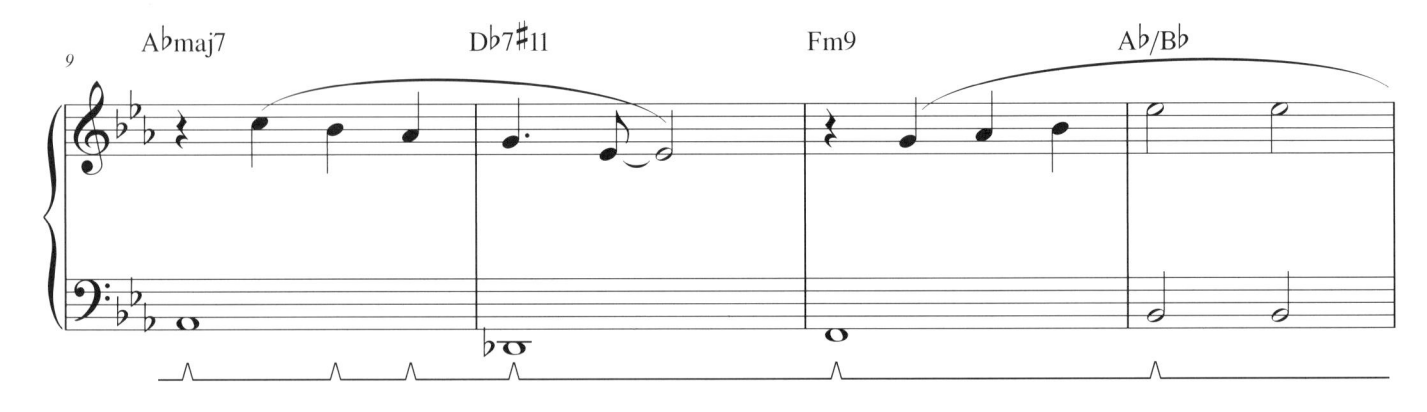

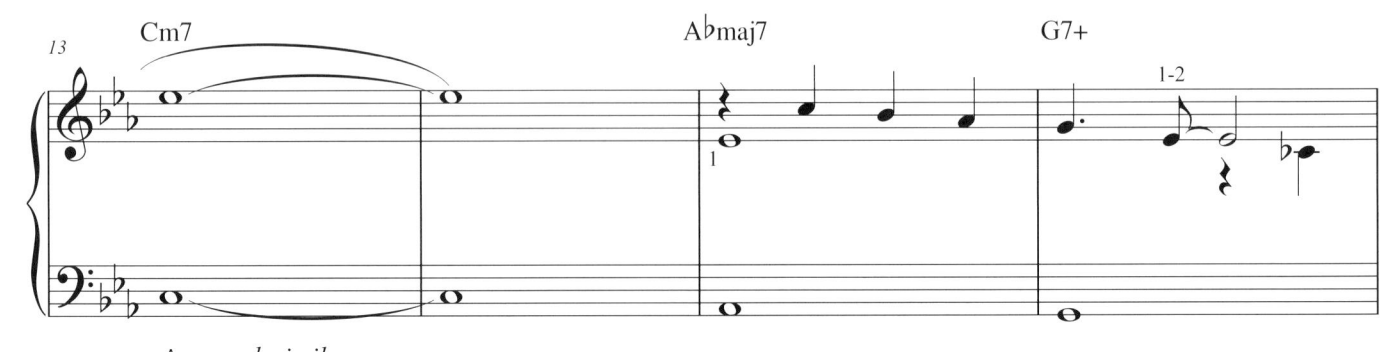

Wayne Hawkins

17
G♭maj7
Fm7
E♭maj7
20
Cm7
Gm7
A♭maj7
24
D♭7
Fm9
A♭/B♭
E♭
28
A♭maj7
mp
G7+
mf
31
G♭maj9
Fm7
E♭maj9

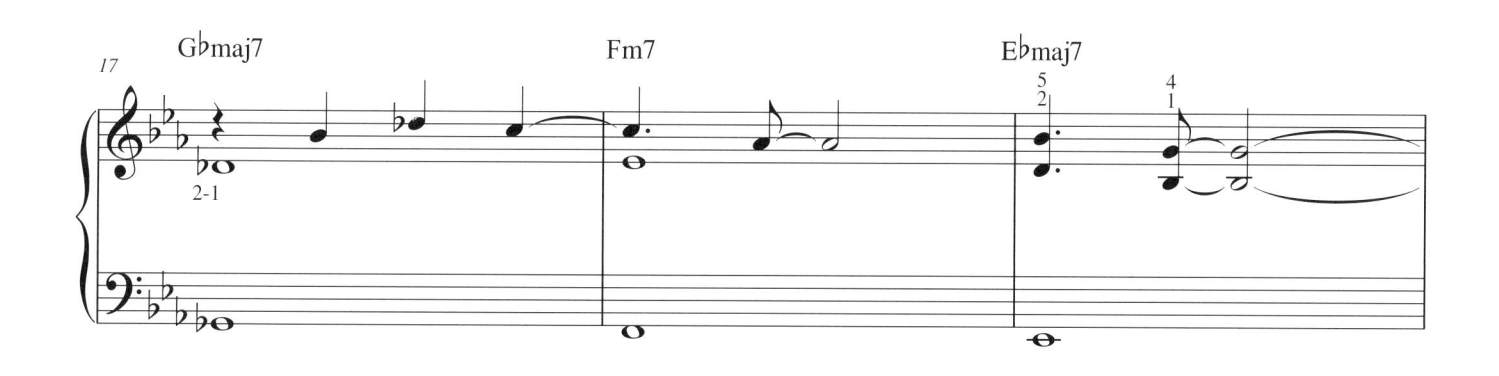

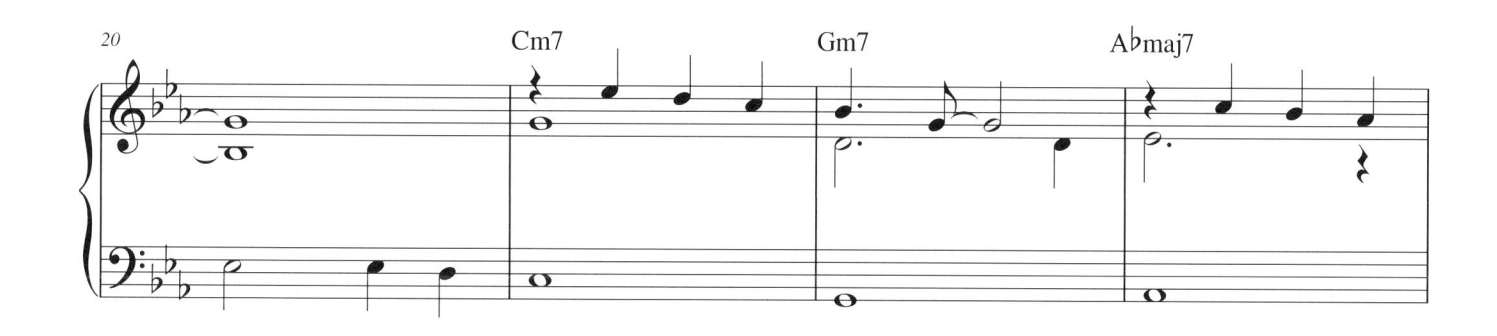

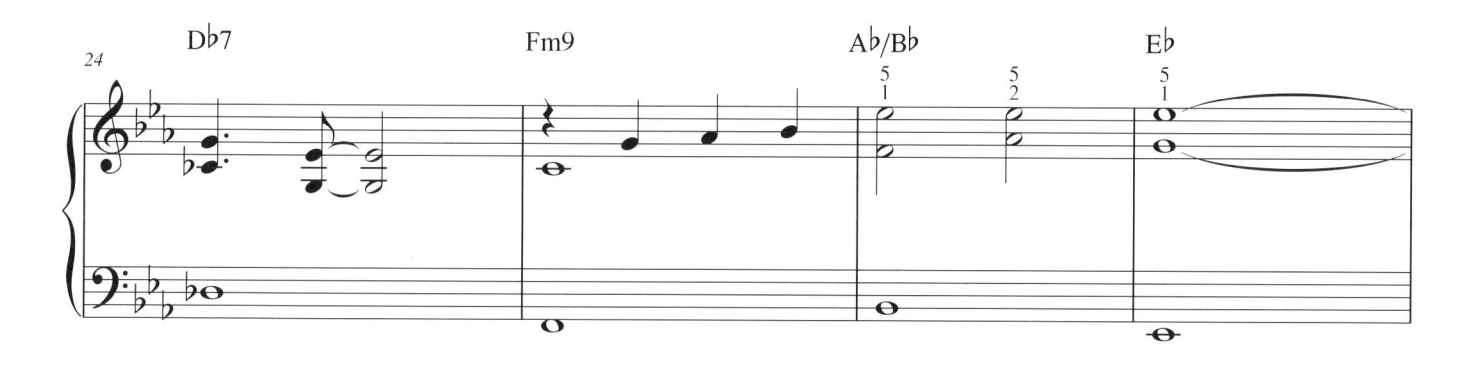

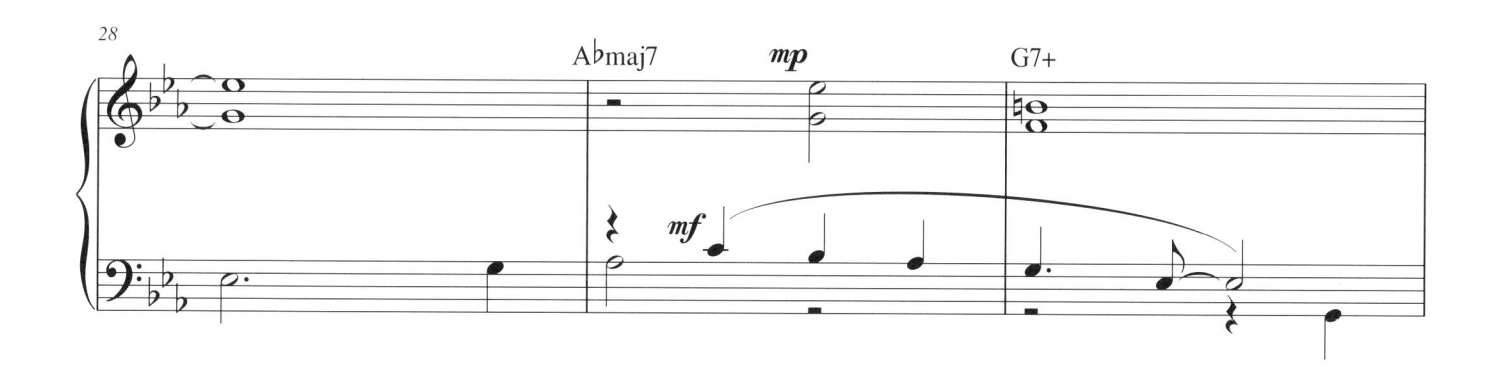

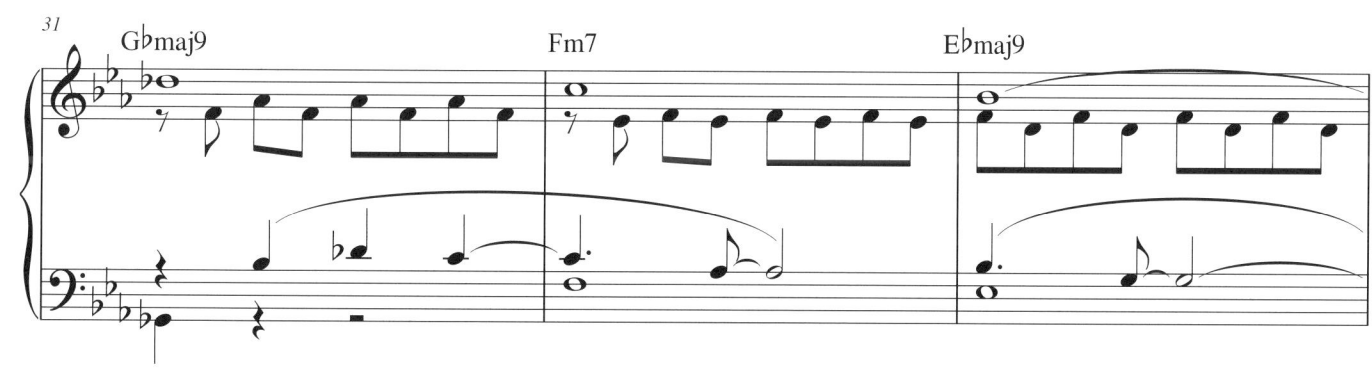

PIANO AEROBICS

WEEKS 13–14

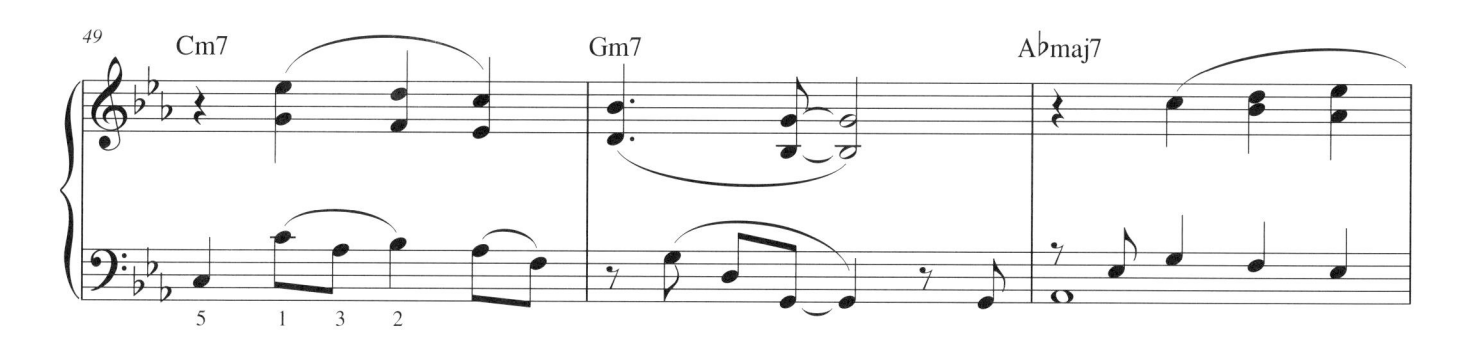

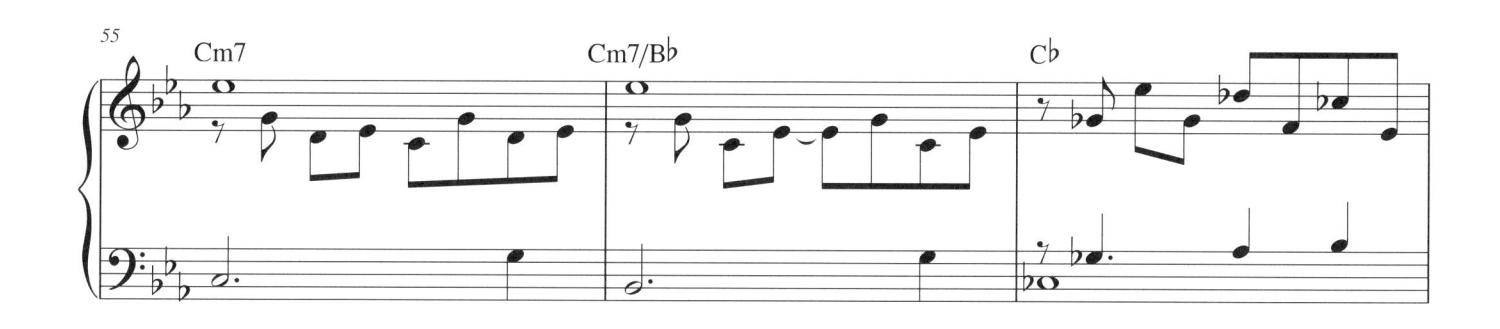

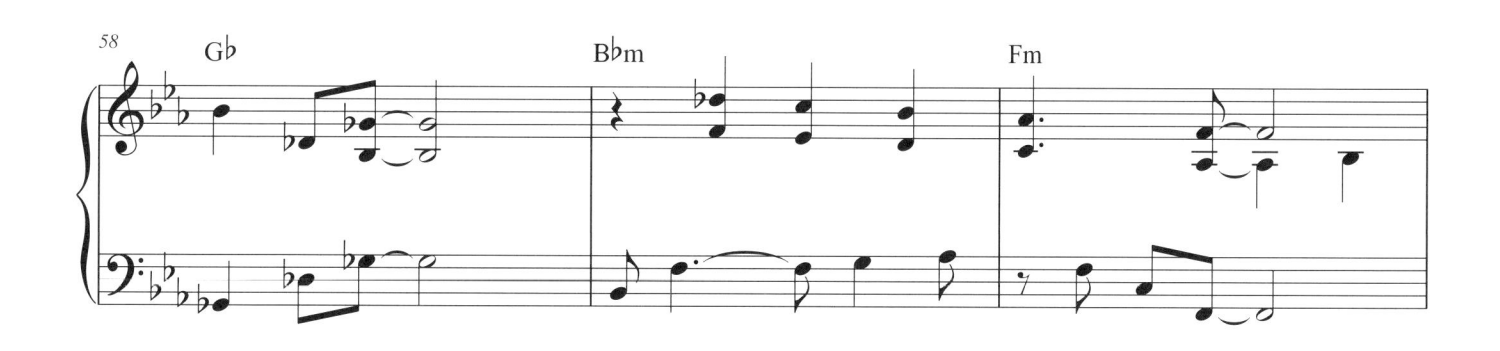

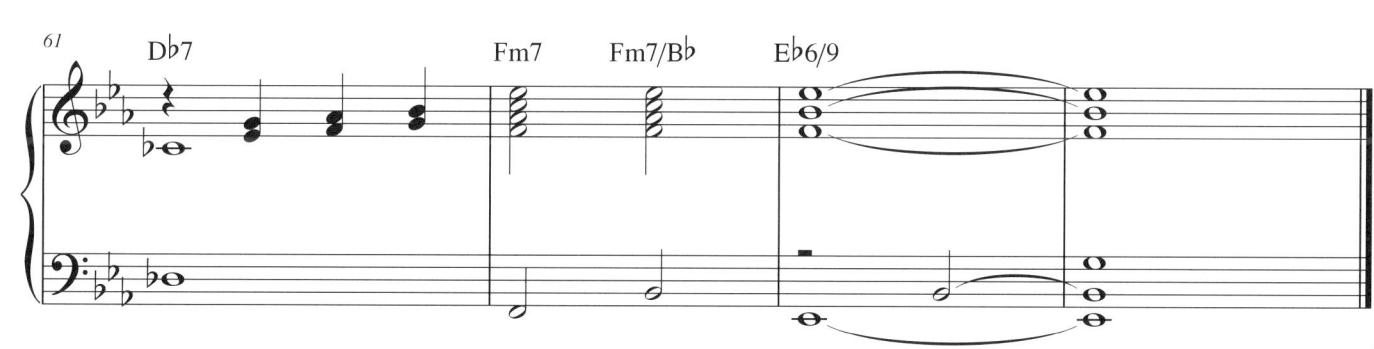

WEEKS 15-16
STRENGTHENING WEAK FINGERS

Isolating and Strengthening Weak Fingers

Our fingers are always a work in progress. For most of us, three of the five digits have special problems. Since the thumb is short and stubby, it likes to make its presence known mostly in the middle of scale passages. Match the tone quality of the thumb to the other fingers in the exercise below.

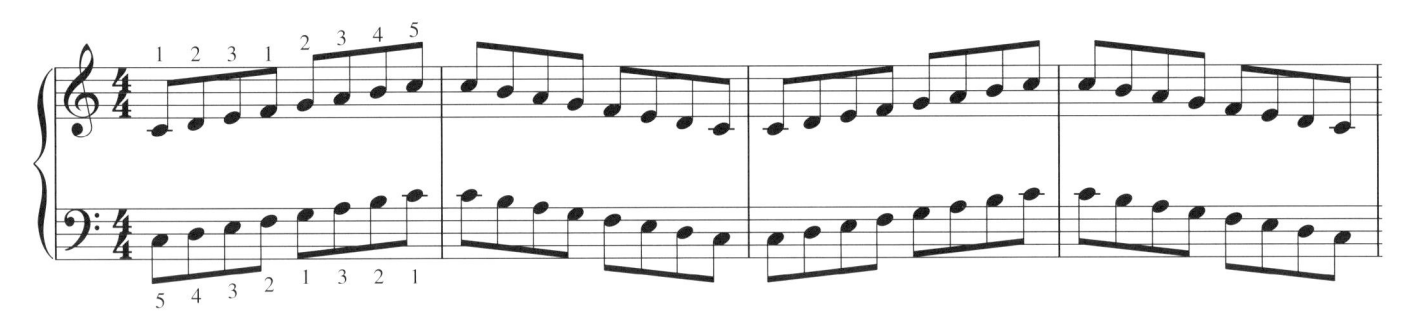

In the figure below, each hand is playing the same melodic line. Because of the shape of each hand, the weak fingers play against the strong fingers. One has to work hard to strengthen the weak fingers to achieve better results.

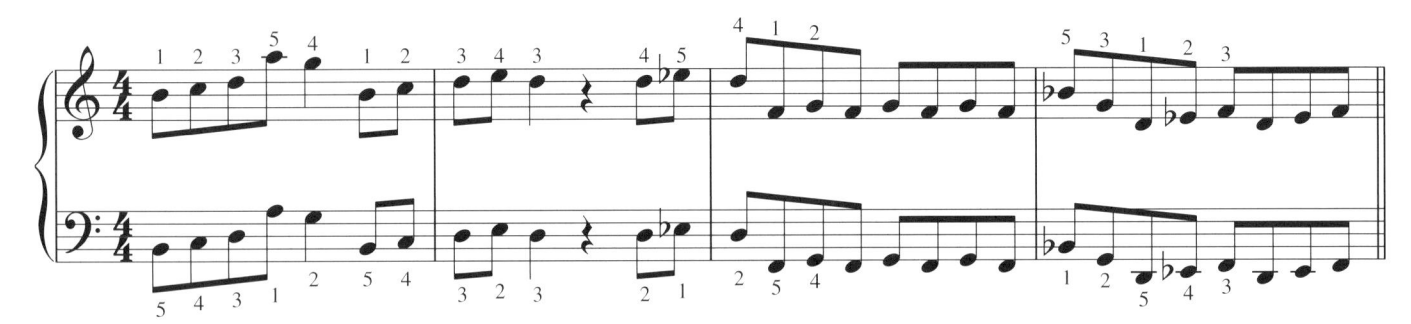

Individual Finger Exercises

These exercises truly isolate the fingers. It is important to be patient and play slowly. As with all of these strengthening exercises, one must lift the fingers as high as possible.

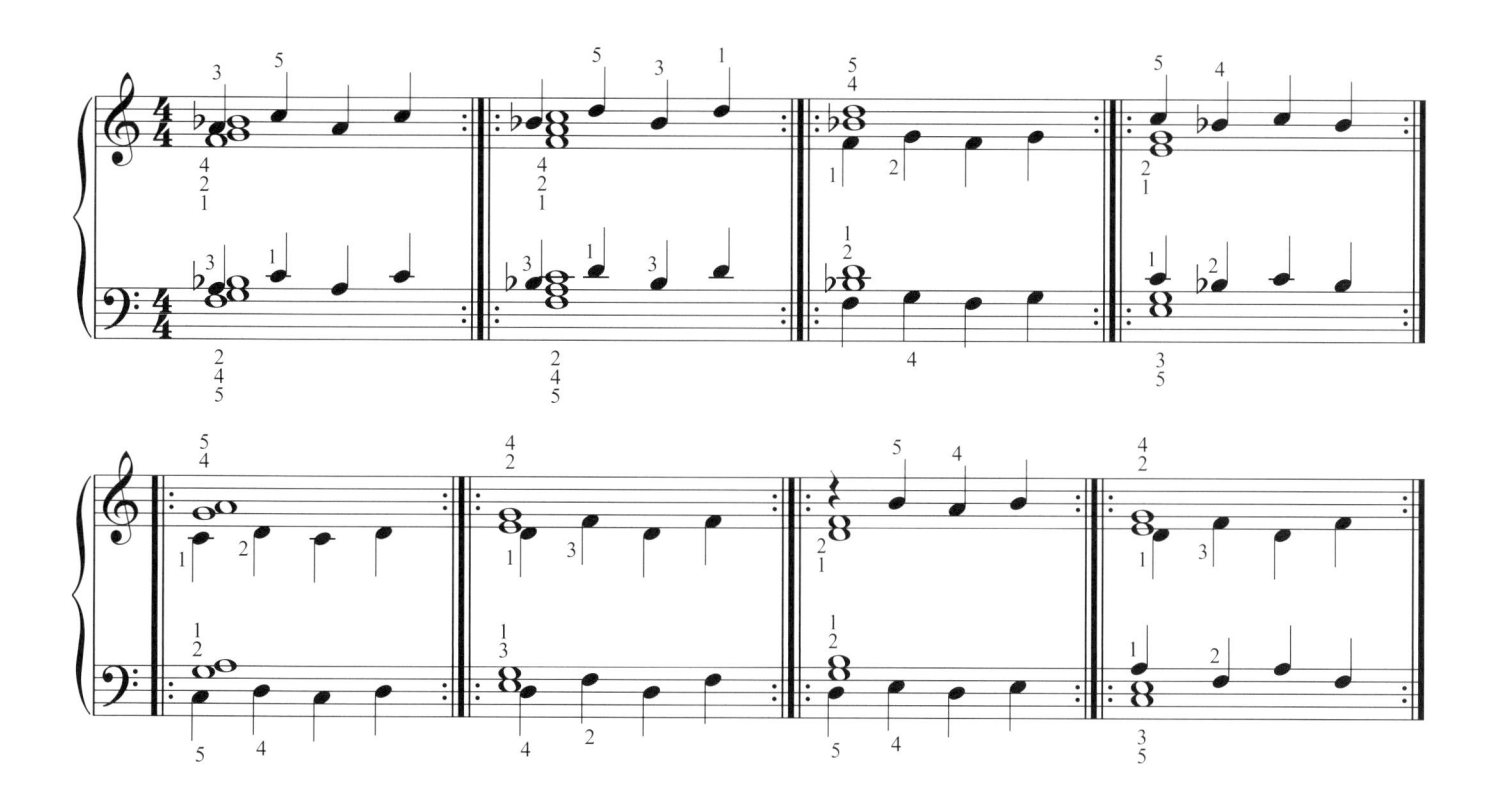

FINGER STRENGTHENING WORKOUT #2

Wayne Hawkins

mp
f

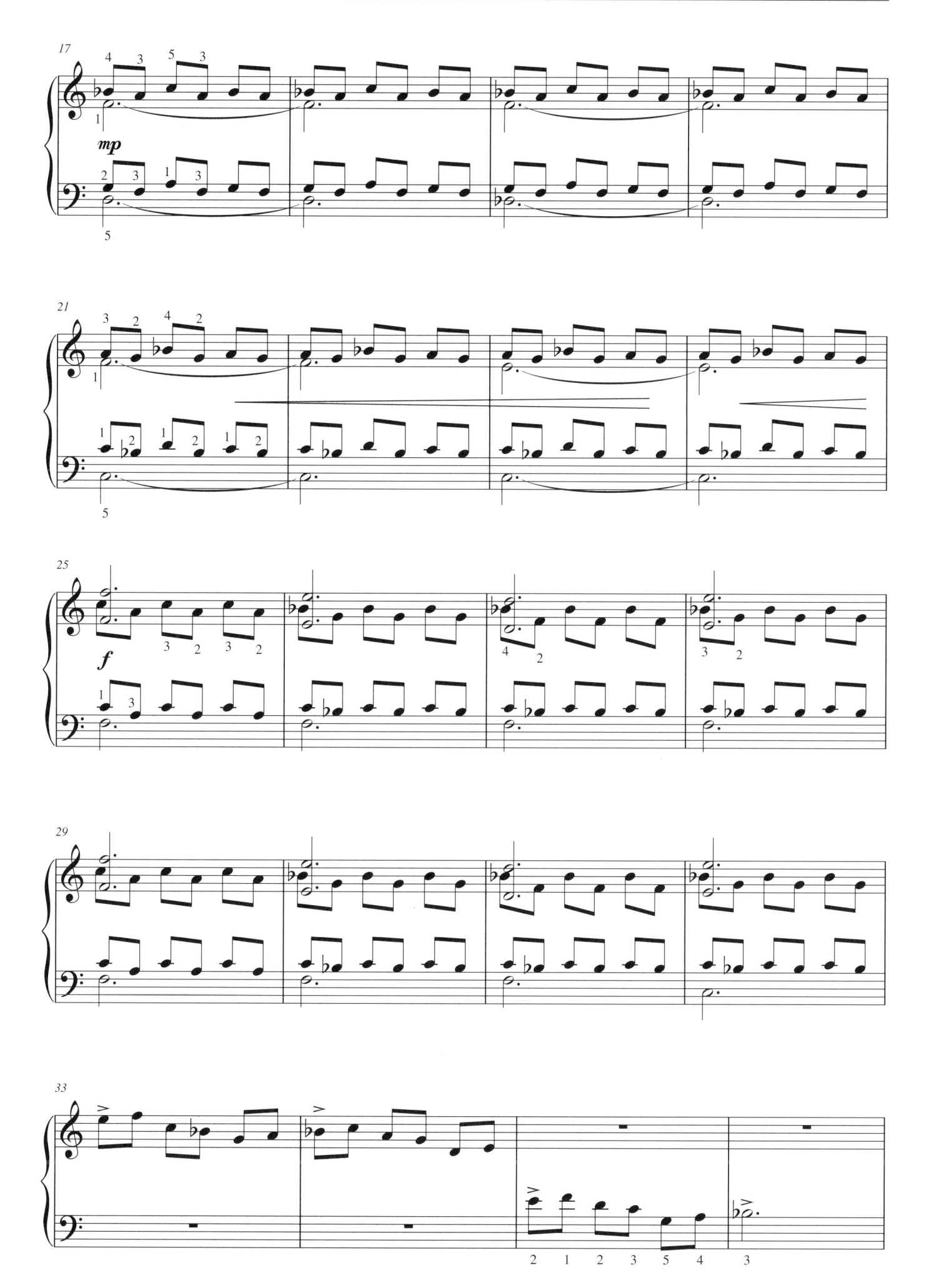

PIANO AEROBICS

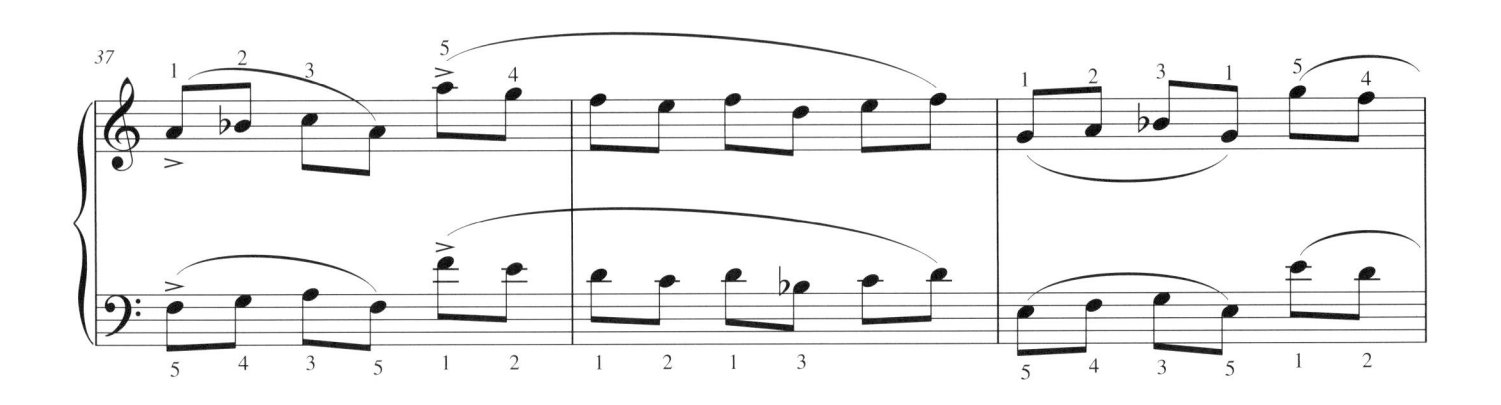

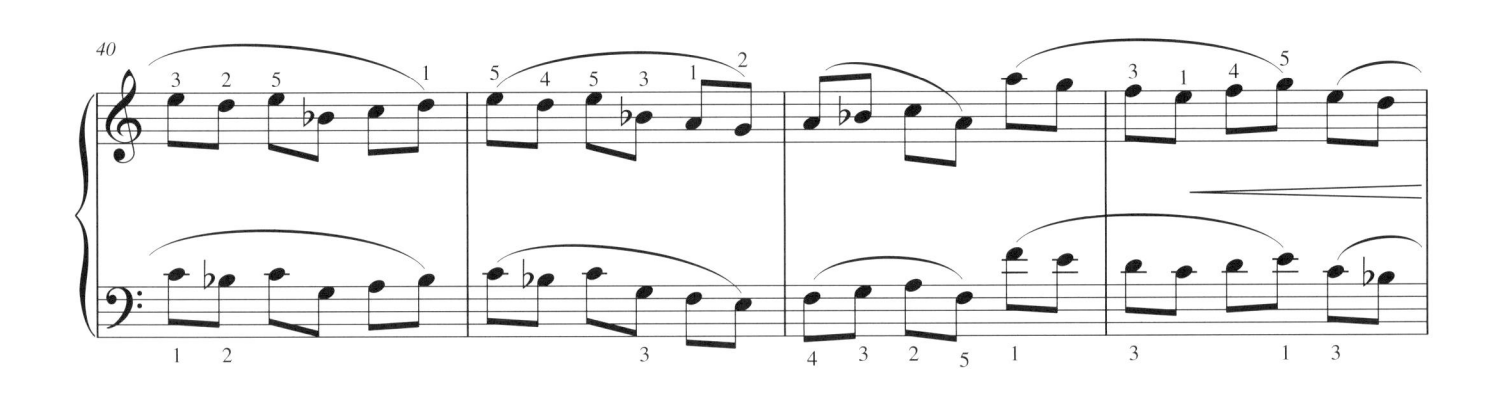

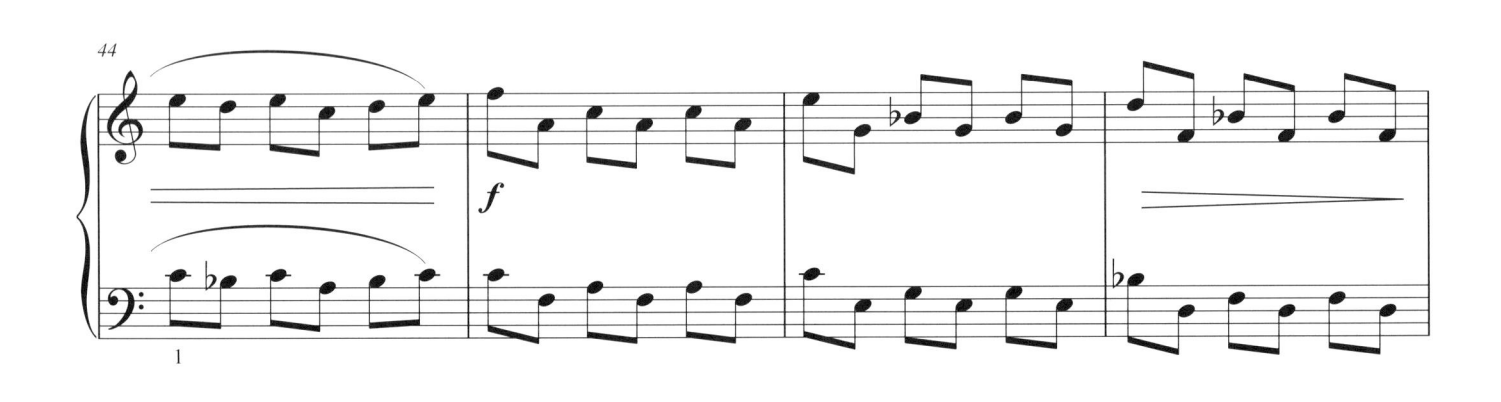

WEEKS 17-18

BOSSA NOVA

Introduction to the Style

In the late 1950s, a new style of music became popular in Brazil. For a short time, it grew into an international phenomenon. This style is called Bossa Nova (or "Bossa"), which means "a new approach" or "new way." This new style combined elements of samba, West Coast Jazz, and an overall more laid back, gentle approach. The Bossa Nova rose to an international phenomenon following a concert at Carnegie Hall in New York in 1962. Featured in this concert were the founding fathers of this style, including Antonio Carlos Jobim. This genre is still popular in Brazil and has long been a staple of jazz and other popular forms.

Rhythmic Syncopation Exercises

The Bossa Nova uses rhythmic patterns to define the style. This is one of the many patterns typically used in Bossa Nova.

1. Play this pattern with a metronome (quarter note = 120). Start by playing each measure individually, then play them together.

2. Bossa Novas and the older cousin of the Bossa Nova, the Samba, are usually felt rhythmically in 2. Example #1 was written in 4/4 to help feel the beat division. Play the revised pattern below in 2/2.

3. After mastering this pattern, it's time to tackle some examples from the workout. In the example below, your right hand is playing with the pattern.

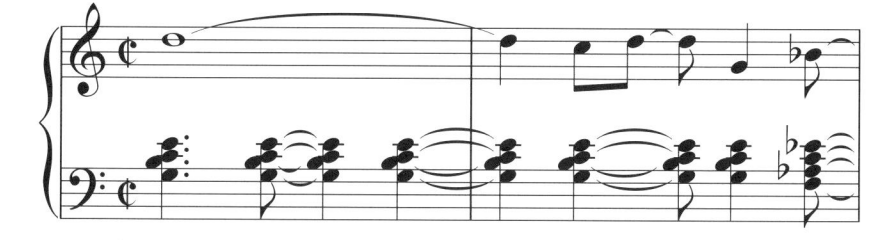

4. In the next example, the melody has a contrasting rhythm.

BOSSA NOVA WORKOUT

TRACK 9

Wayne Hawkins

Laid back, smooth (♩ = 100)

WEEKS 17–18

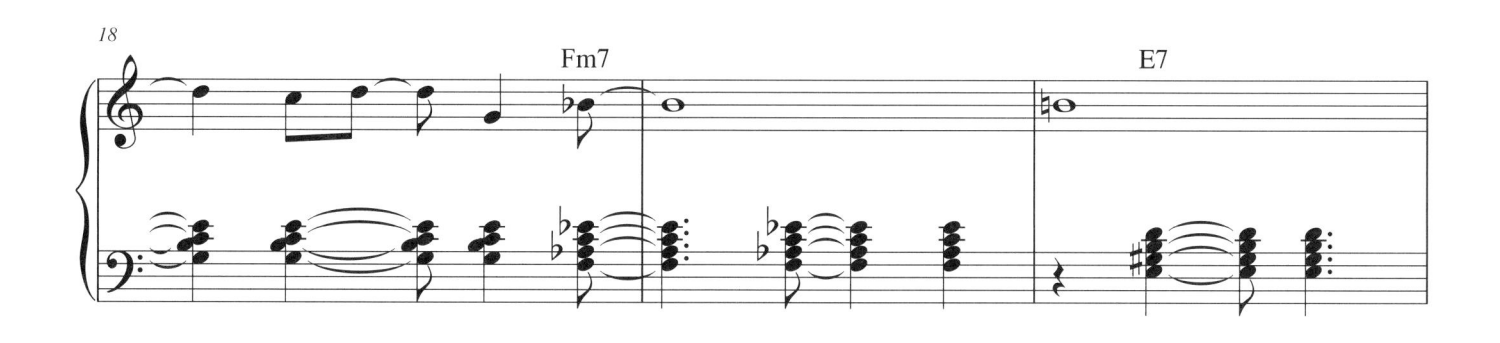

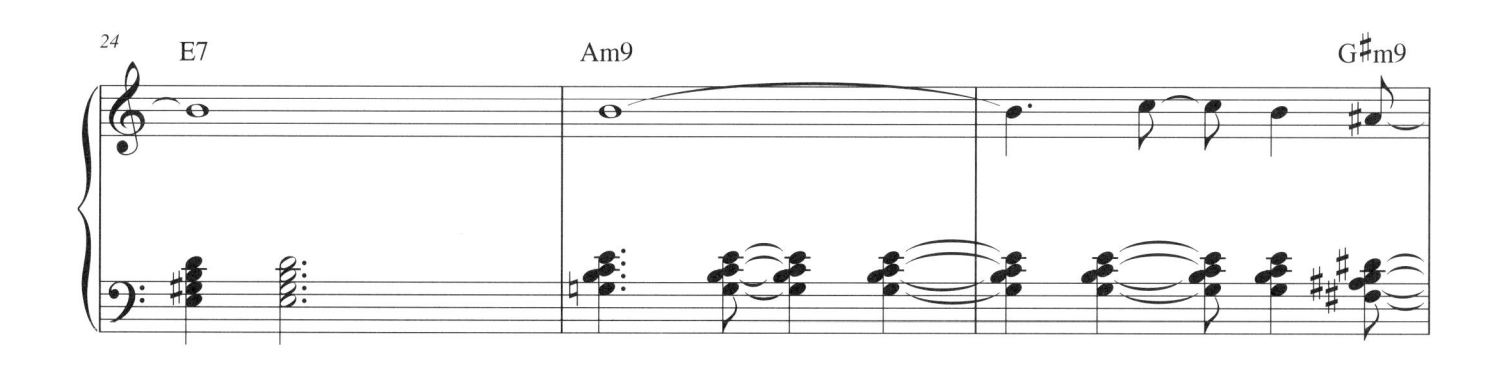

PIANO AEROBICS

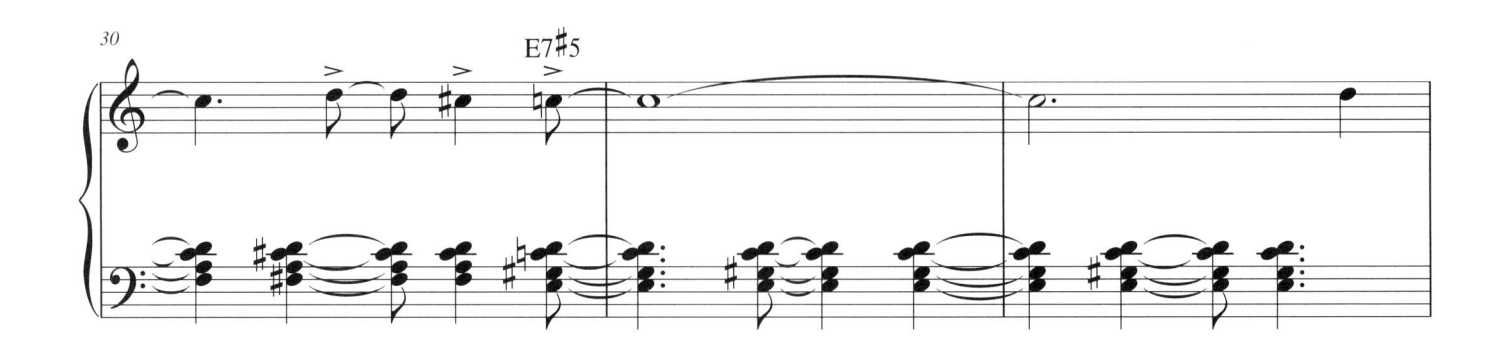

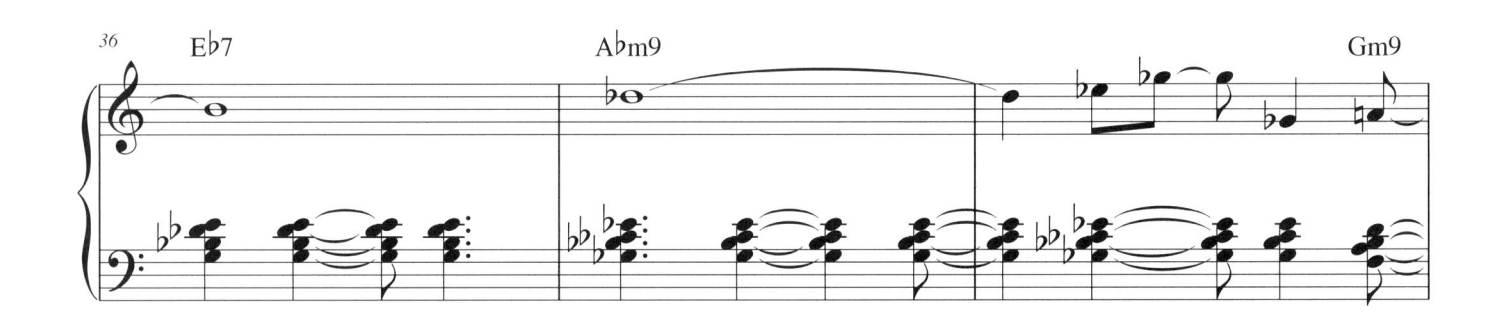

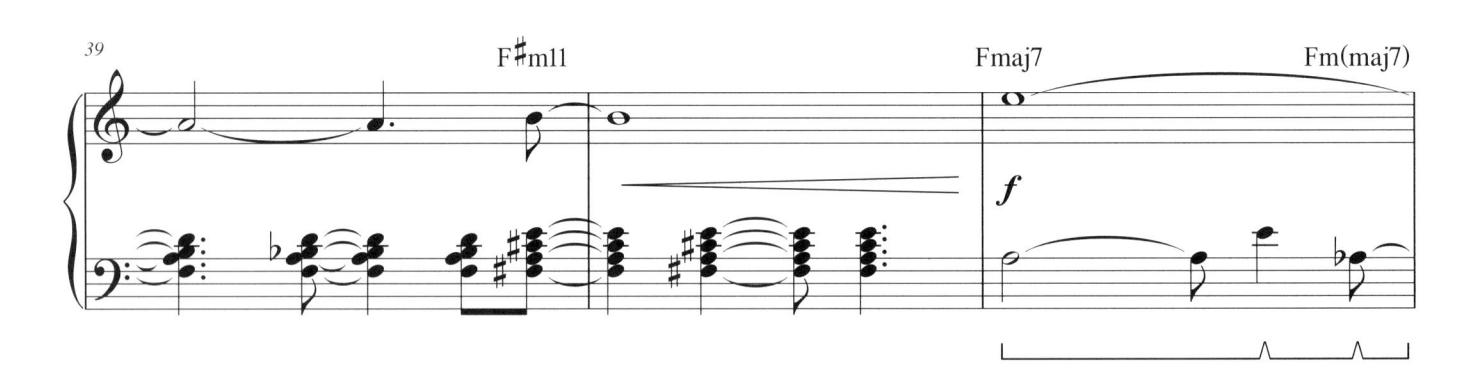

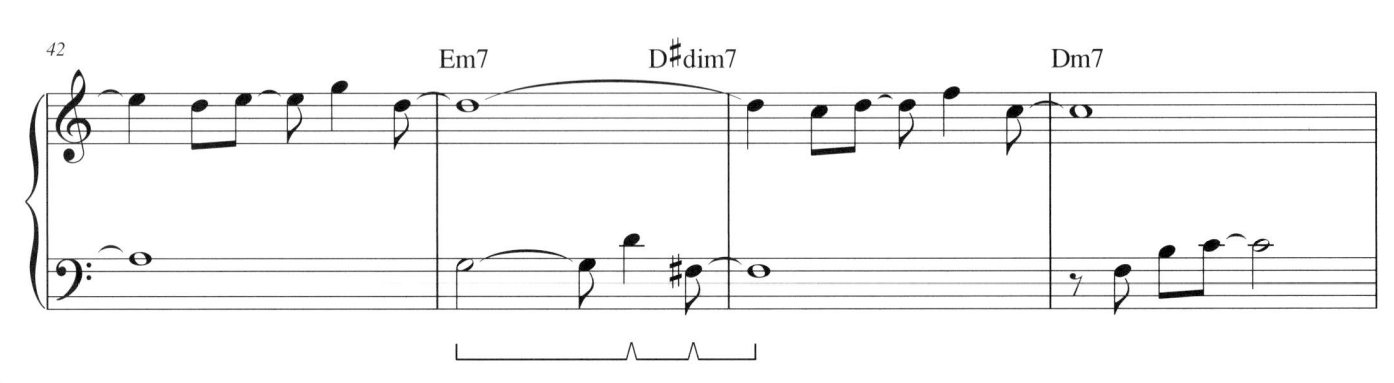

46
D♯dim7
Em7
F♯dim7
Fmaj7
Fm(maj7)
50
Em7
D♯m7
Dm7
D♯dim7
54
Cmaj7/E
D♯dim7
decresc.
57
Dm7
E7♯5
Am7
mp
61
Am9
pp

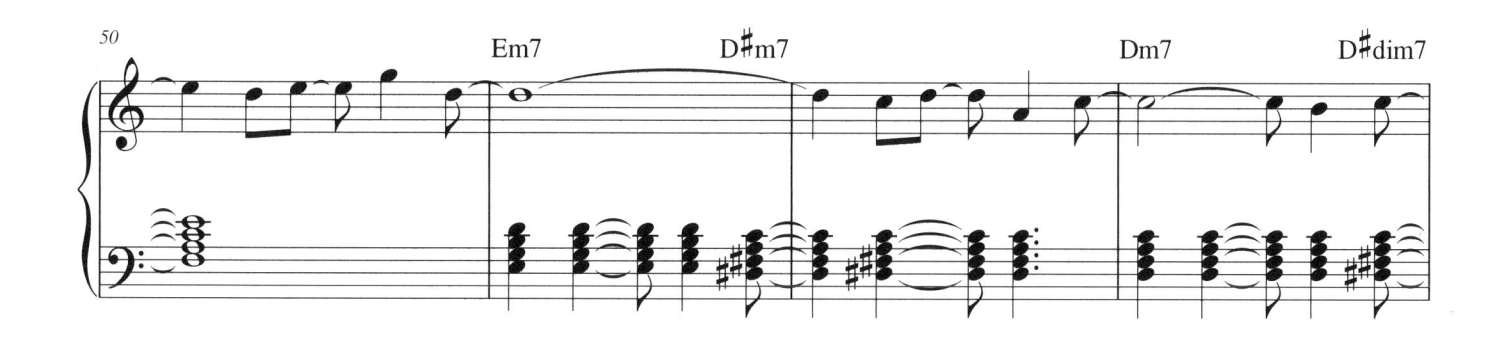

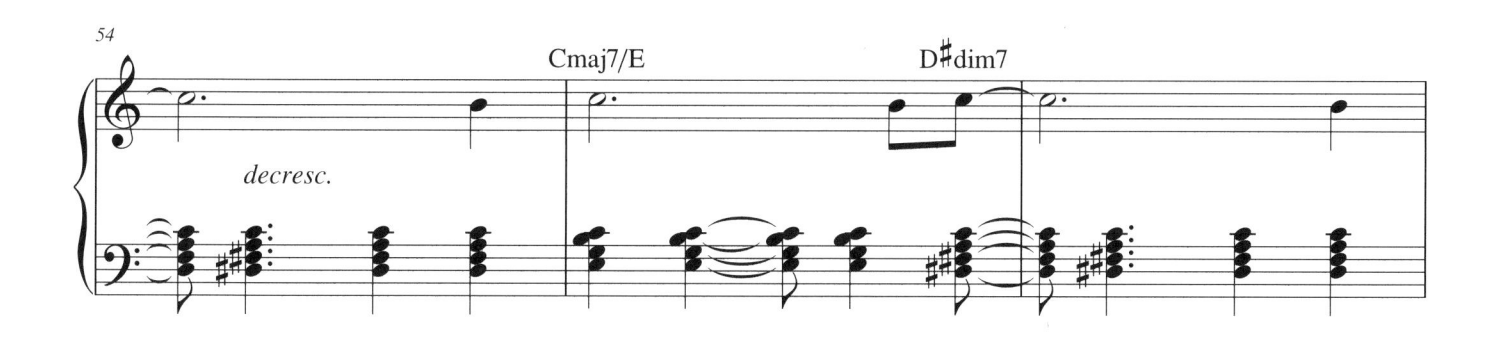

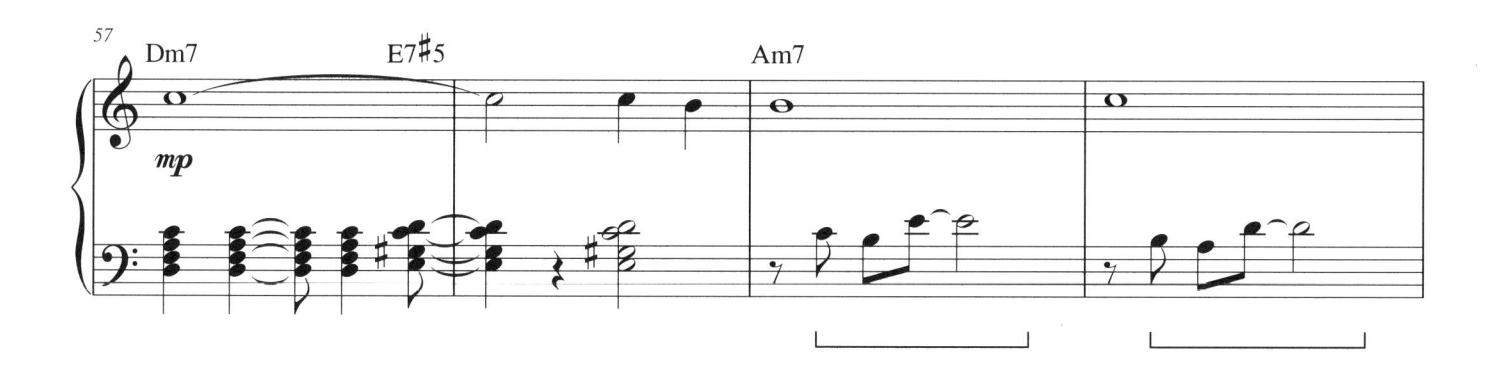

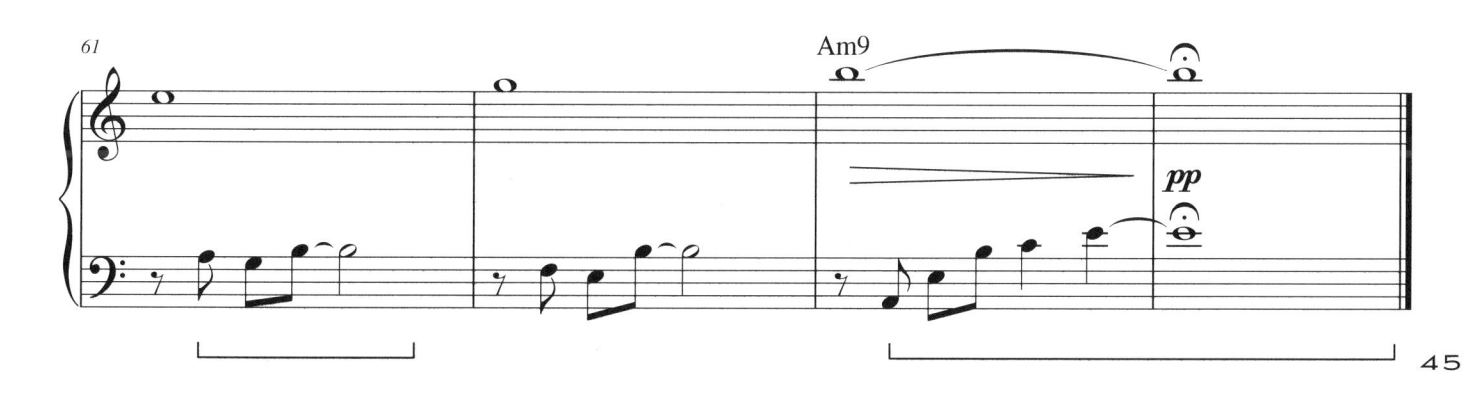

WEEKS 19-20

ACCOMPANYING

Rhythm Playing Versus Solo Playing

A complete keyboard player should be able to accompany as well as playing solo. In big bands, choral ensembles, or other combos, a keyboard player needs to accompany the other instruments and/or voices. Rhythm playing, such as accompanying, requires a commitment to playing a steady groove. Solo playing requires a different mindset.

Vertical Reading Exercises

Playing for choirs or in bands requires some skill at vertical reading.

1. Play the example below.

The best way to acquire the skill of vertical reading is by accompanying choirs and regularly playing multiple-part harmony.

At first, this chord might seem hard to read.

2. Look at the example below.

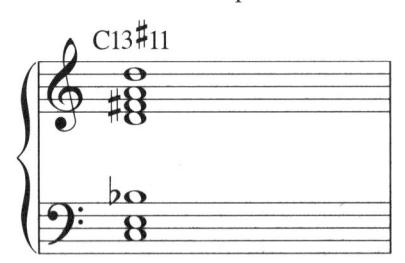

3. The same chord is in this example.

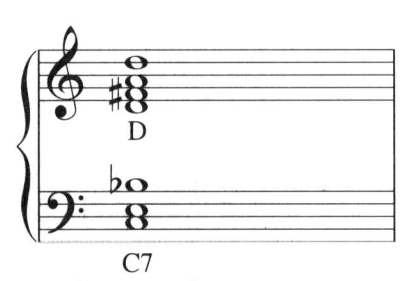

4. If you look at this as two different harmonic chords, it seems easier to read.

Another method is to arpeggiate each chord before attempting to play the chords together. As you continue into the Vertical Reading Workout, take time to try the methods described above to assist you in reading.

VERTICAL READING WORKOUT

Wayne Hawkins

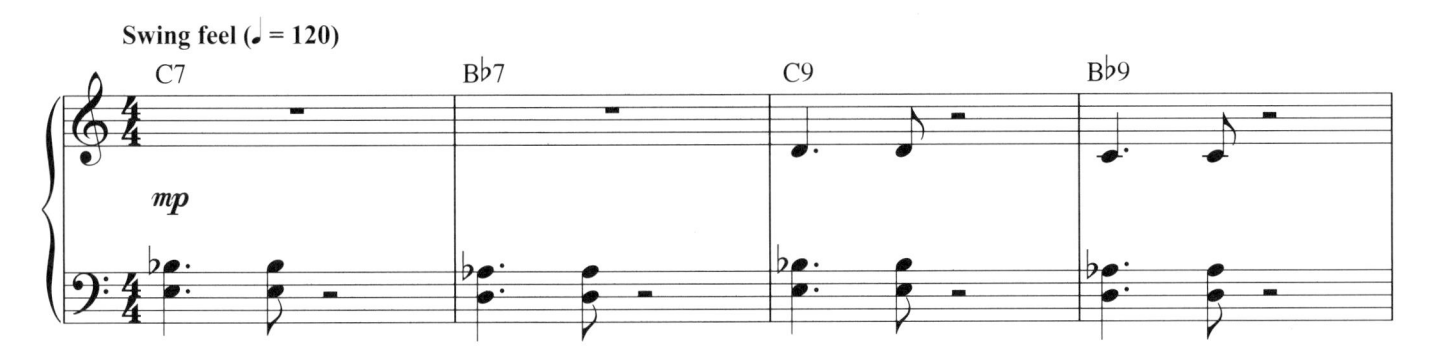

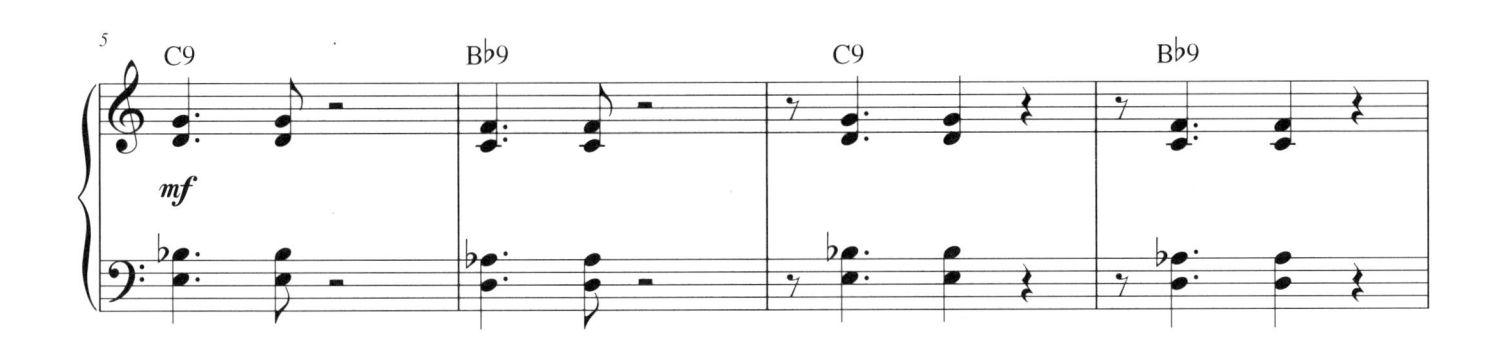

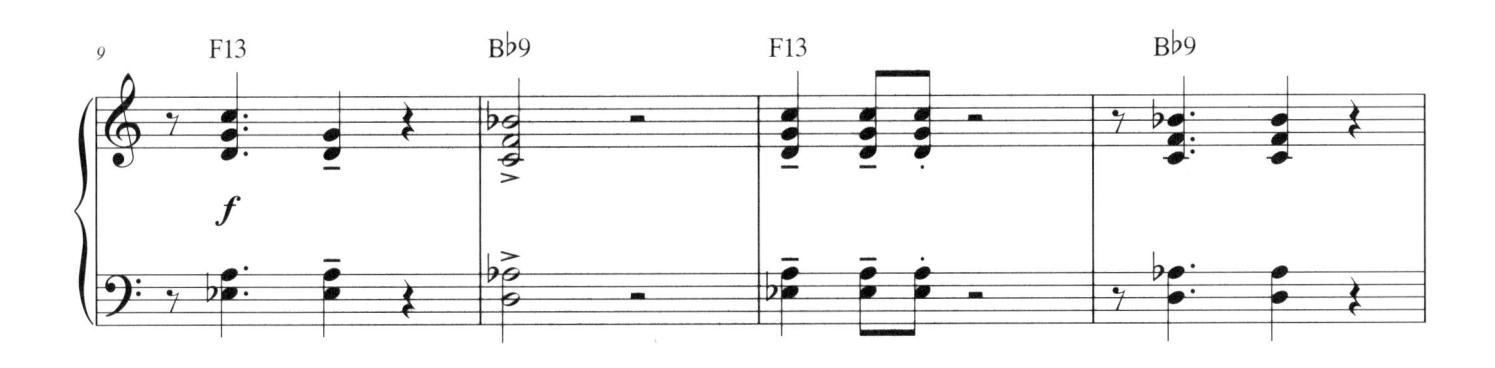

PIANO AEROBICS

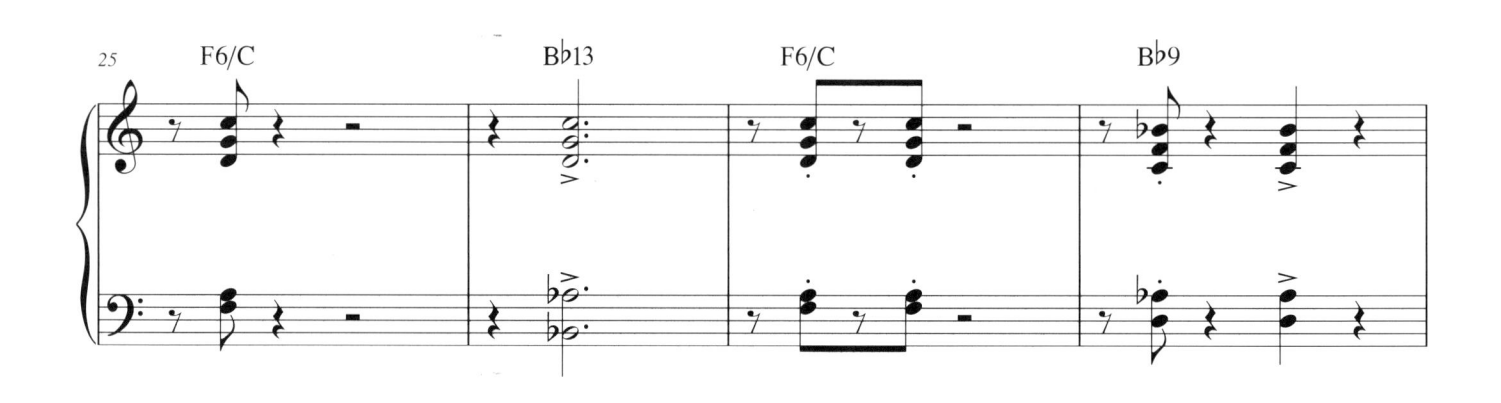

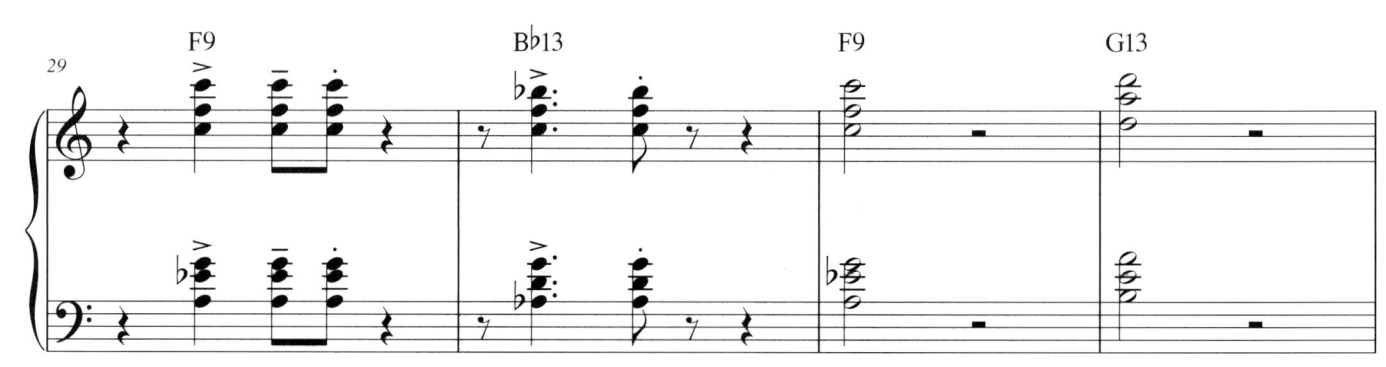

WEEKS 19–20

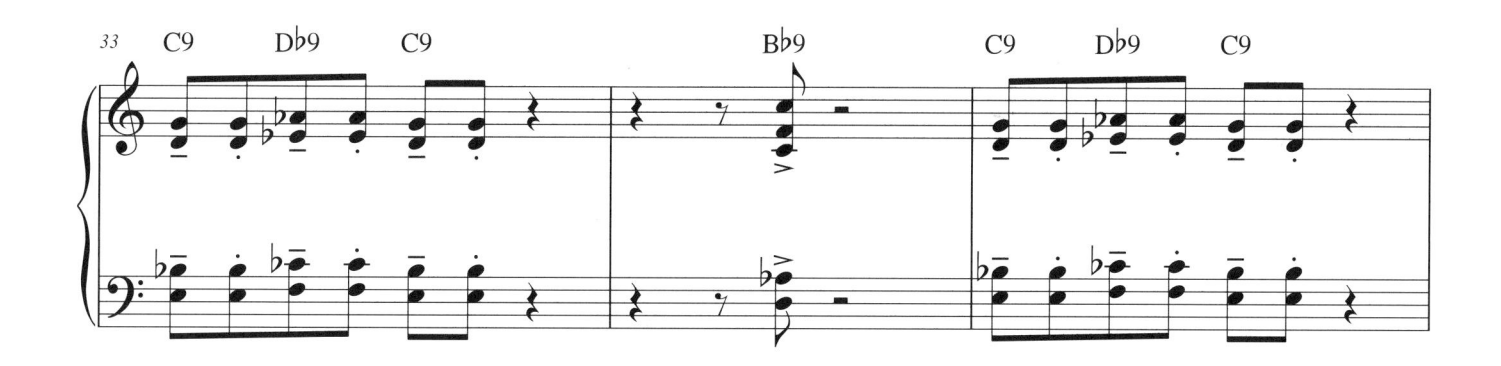

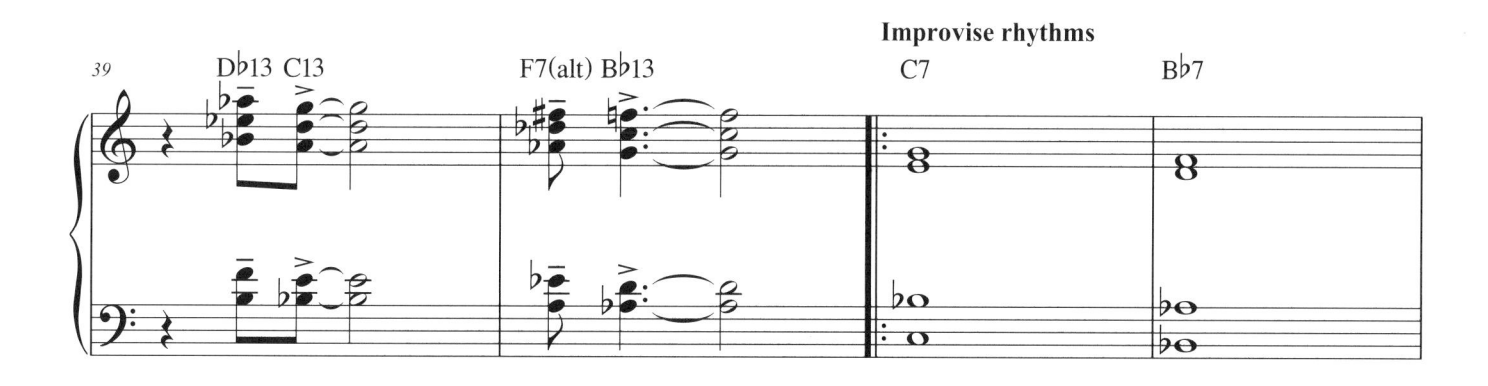

WEEKS 21-22

USE OF THE THUMB

All (About) Thumbs

One of the biggest challenges in playing the piano lies in the fact that our fingers are not the same size. Often in scale passages we are reminded of that fact, especially when using the thumb. It is the "stump" of the hand and can be somewhat inflexible. There are, however, ways to adapt the thumb so that your hand can play scales more evenly.

1. Play the exercises below, using the fingering as indicated. Try to play both as smoothly as possible. Please note that when weight is distributed evenly, each tone has a clear articulation in a legato pattern.

2. Play the C scale below using the fingerings as indicated. Be careful to delay the weight shift until slightly after pressing the key with the thumb.

3. Try this exercise with the left hand.

4. Play the exercise below with the left hand, using the fingerings as indicated.

5. Play the C scale below with the left hand. Again, be careful to delay the weight shift until slightly after pressing the key with the thumb.

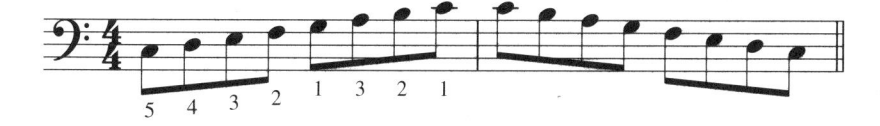

(ALL) THUMBS WORKOUT

Wayne Hawkins

TRACK 11

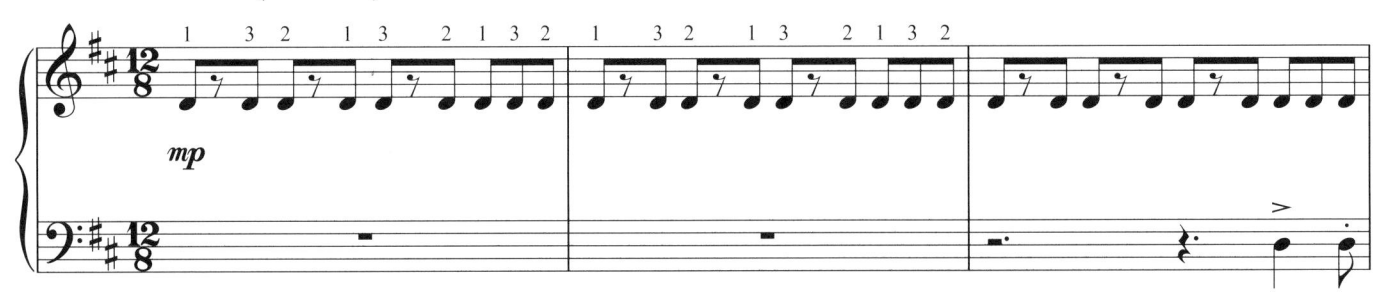

WEEKS 21-22

PIANO AEROBICS

mf
mf
f
ff

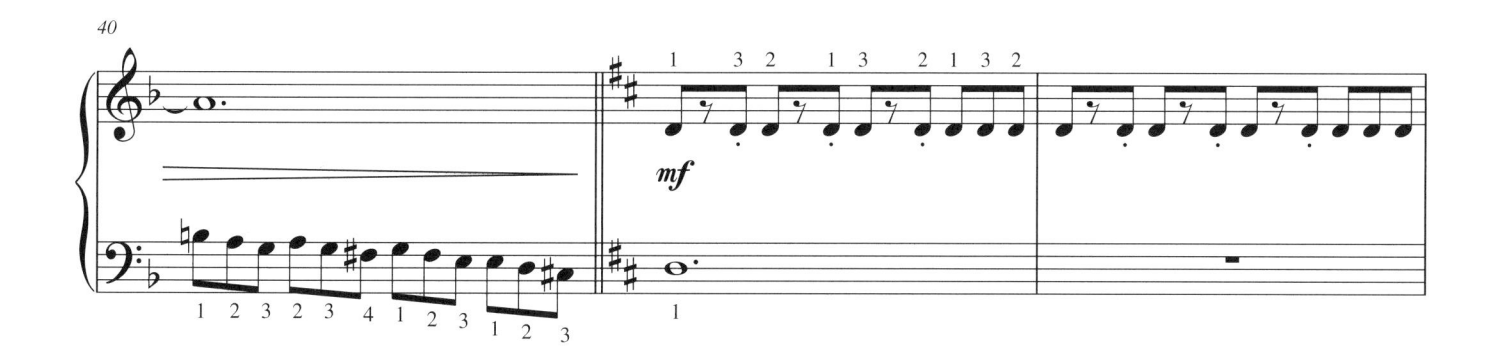

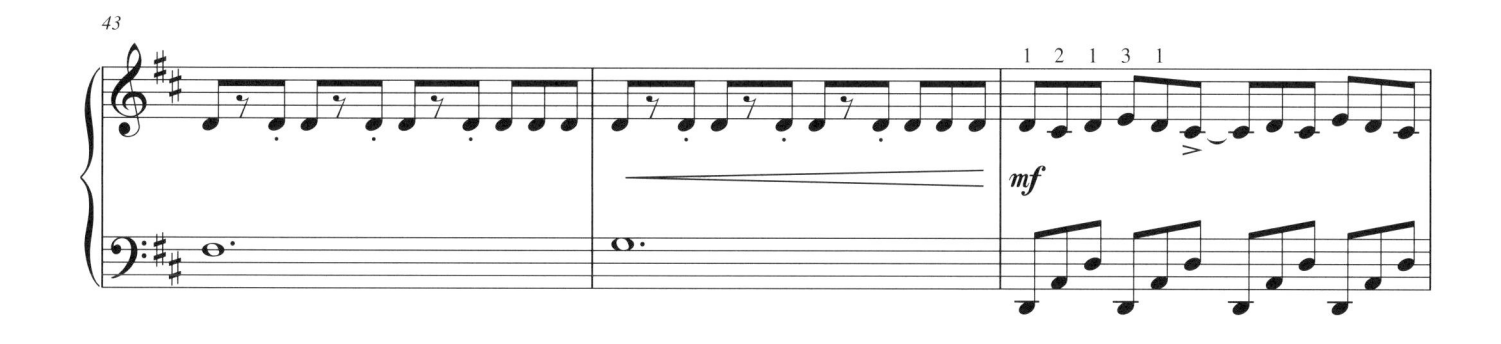

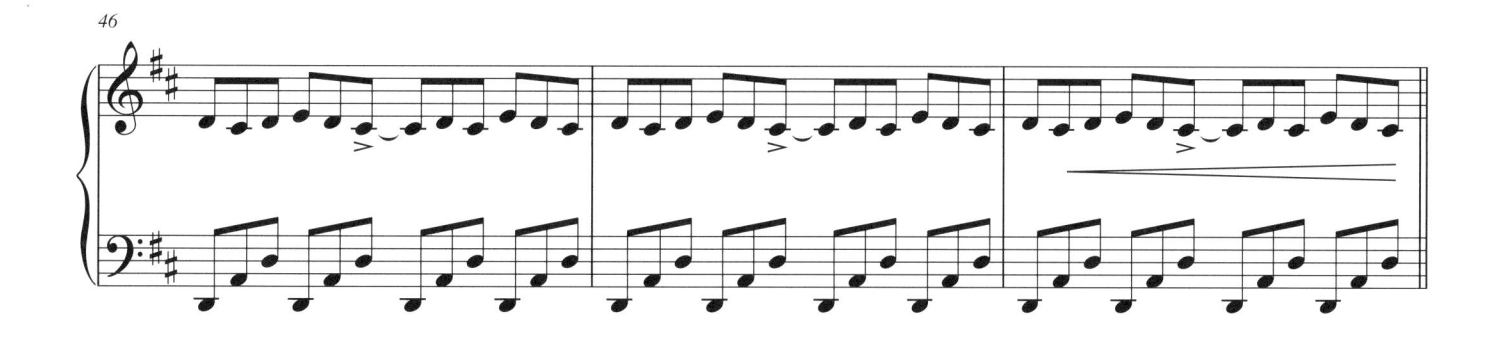

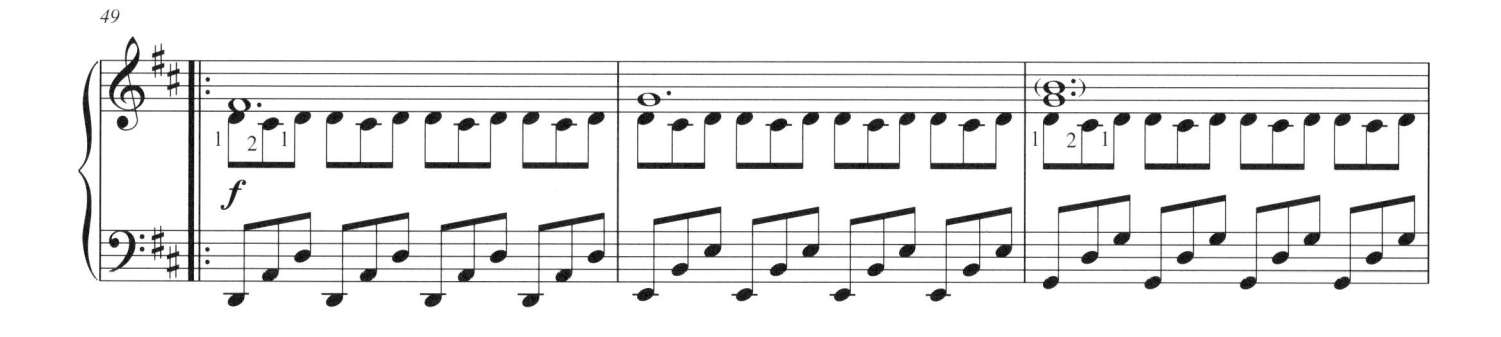

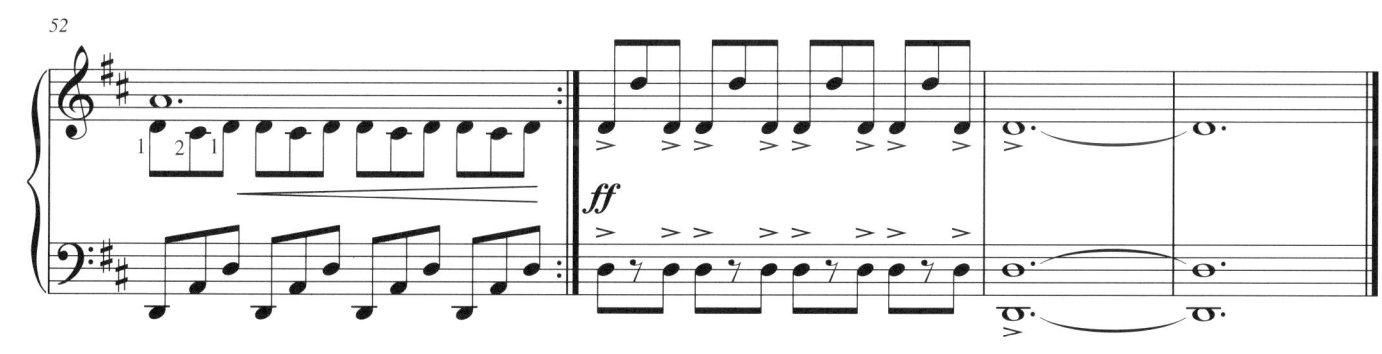

WEEKS 23-24

RELATIONSHIP BETWEEN BLUES AND JAZZ

Comparison Between Blues and Jazz

In this section we will explore the difference between the structure of a typical 12-bar blues and a 12-bar blues used in jazz. Please see the table below for a comparison of the styles.

BLUES	JAZZ
Heavier approach to groove	Lighter approach to groove
Ostinato patterns are riffs	Walking bass instead of riff
Less harmonic movement	More complex harmonies
Less interaction between soloist and rhythm section	More interaction between soloist and rhythm section

Below is a generic 12-bar blues progression. In the parentheses are modified jazz harmonies showing a different progression using the same structure.

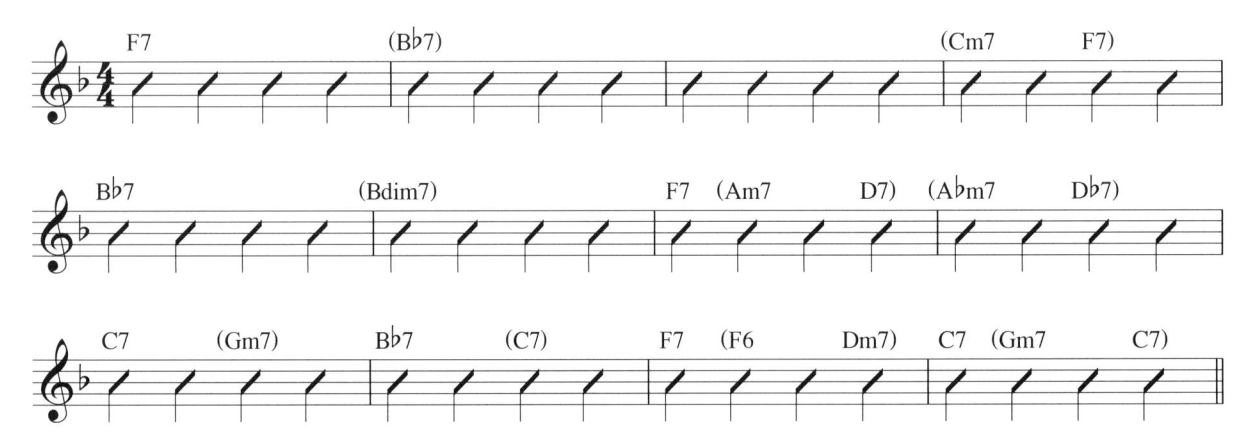

Blues Exercise

This is an example of riff-oriented blues.

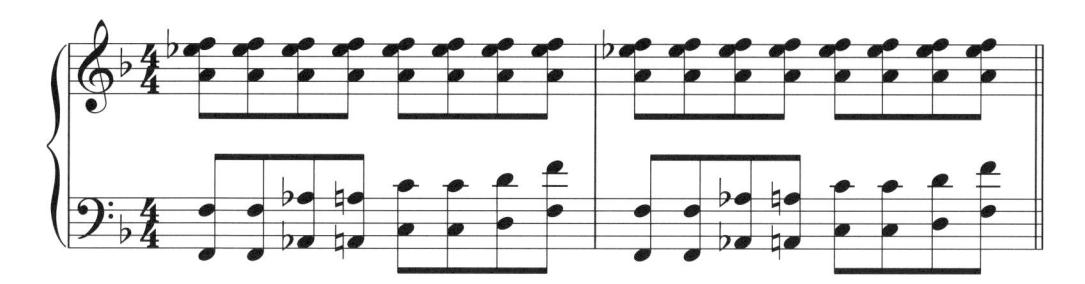

This is an example of a basic shuffle pattern for either a bass player or pianist.

PIANO AEROBICS

BLUES AND JAZZ WORKOUT

TRACK 12

Wayne Hawkins

Bluesy, Swing eighths (♩ = 108)

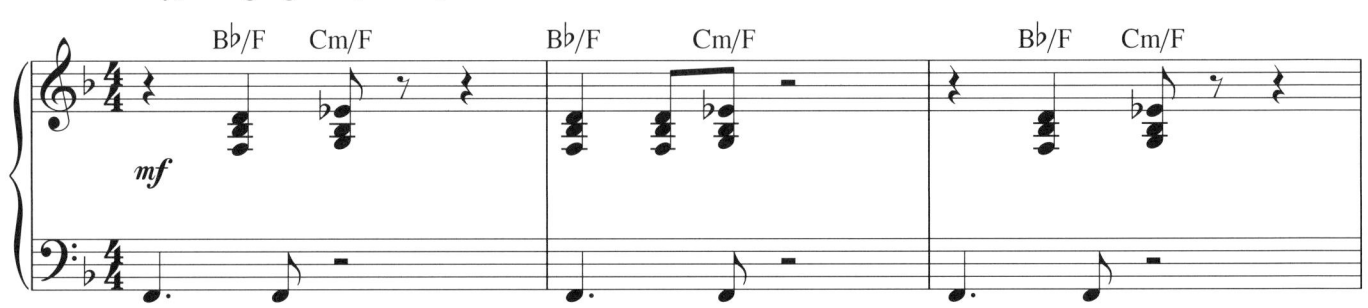

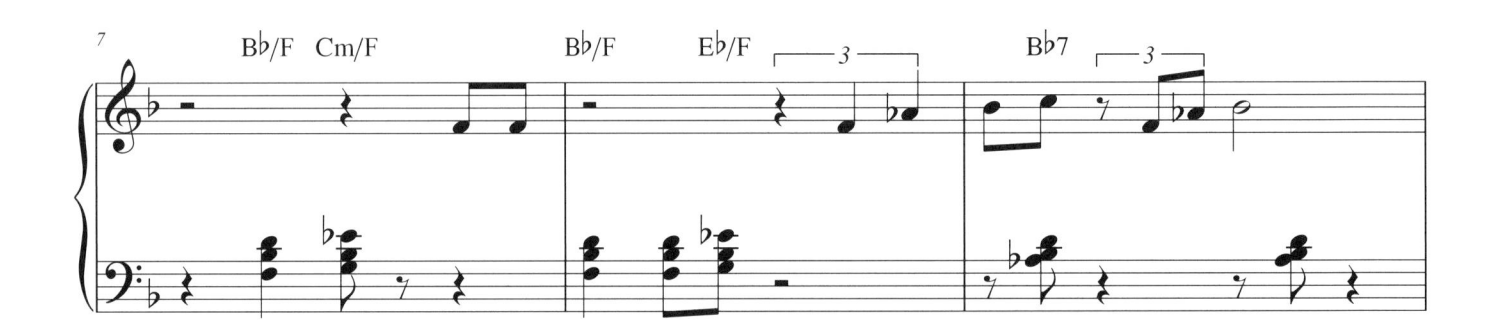

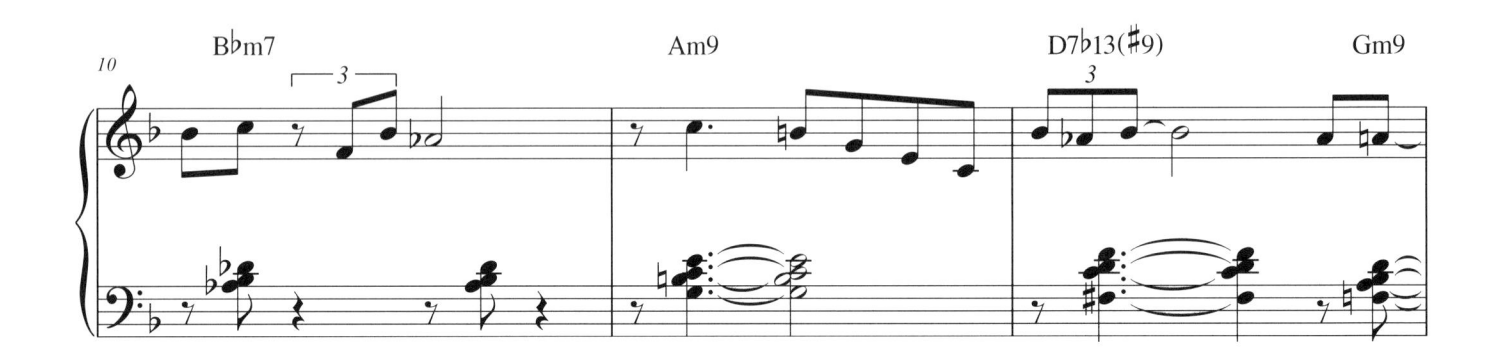

13
C7♭9(♭13)
F7
16
A♭7
G7
G♭7
F7
19
B♭7♭9
22
F7♭13
D♭7
25
C7
B♭7
Am11
A♭m11

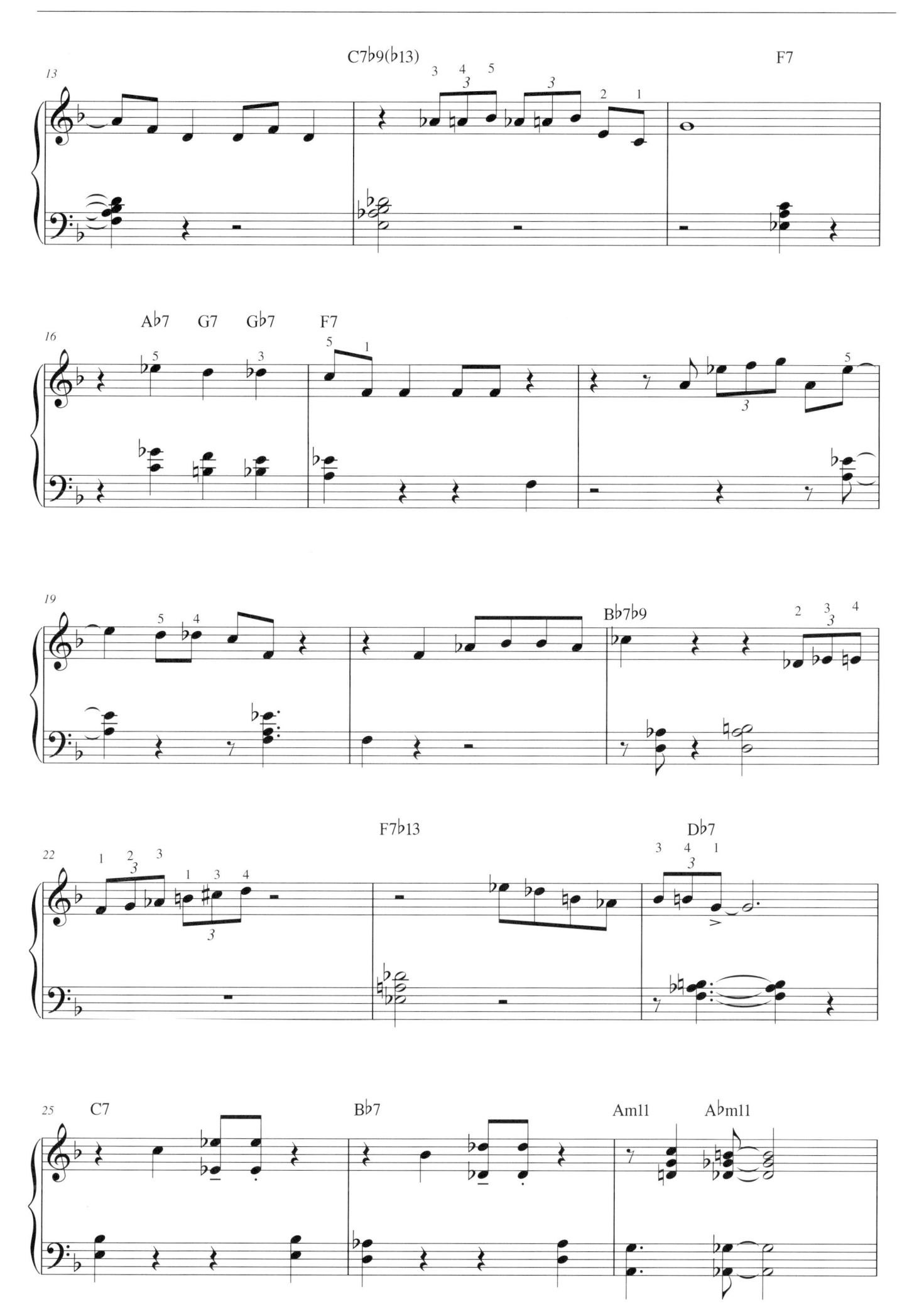

PIANO AEROBICS

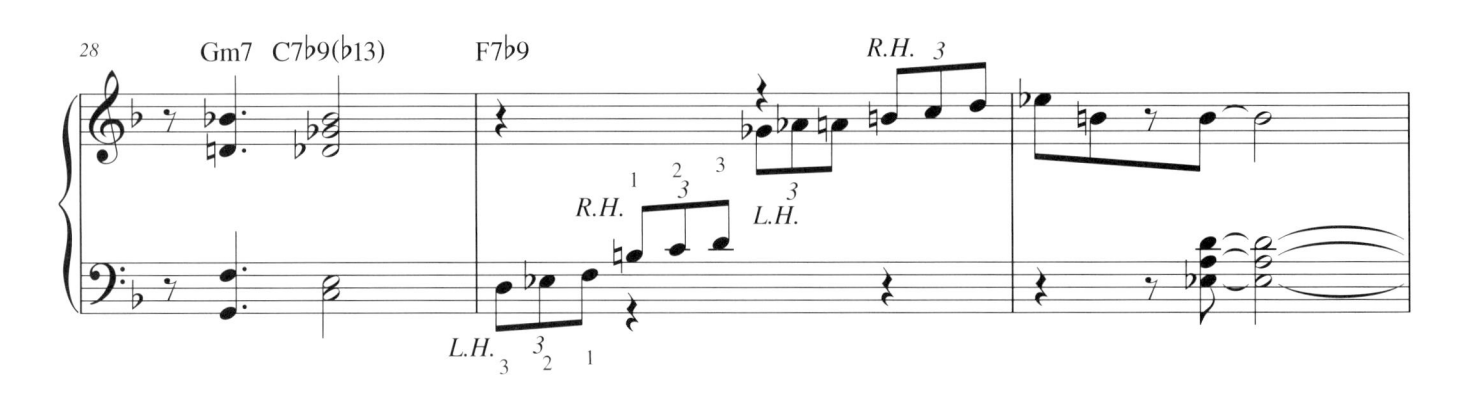

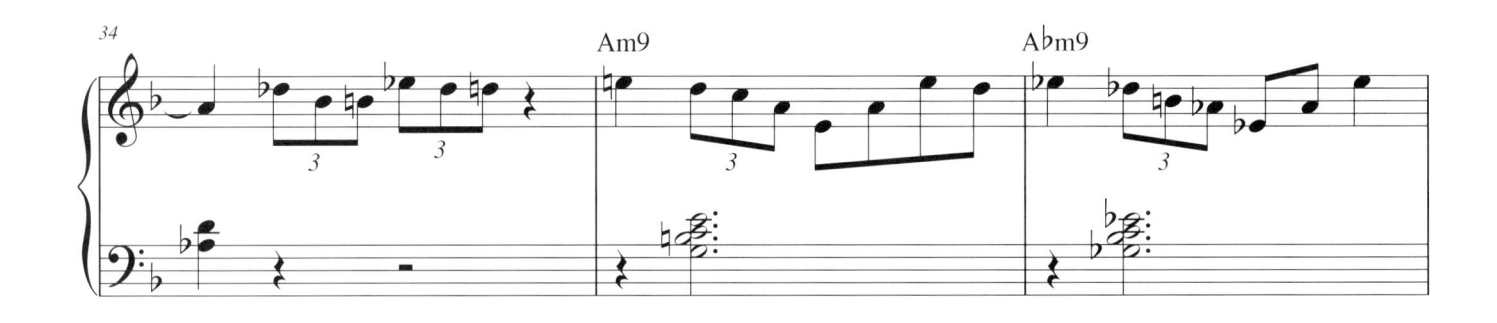

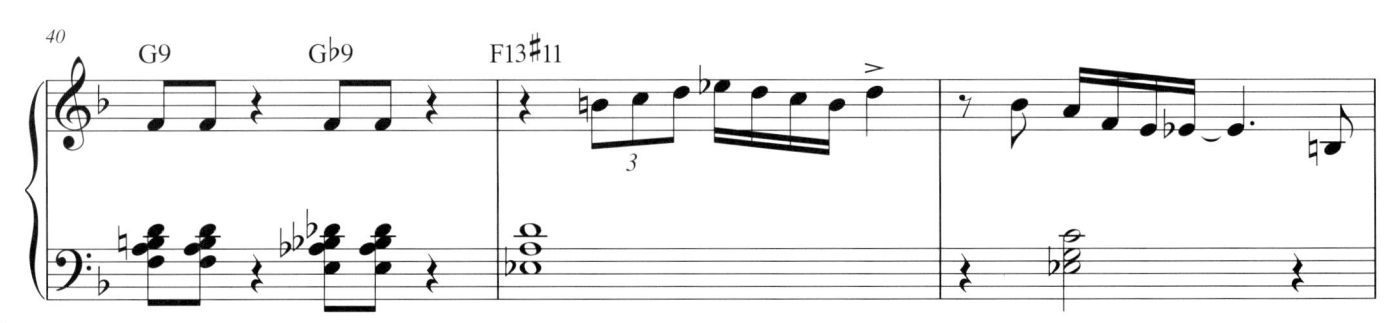

43
B♭7
46
E♭7
Am7
D7♭9
49
Gm9
Am7
B♭6
Csus9
C9
2
(drum fill)
53
F9
E♭9
F9
E♭9
57
F9
E♭9
F13

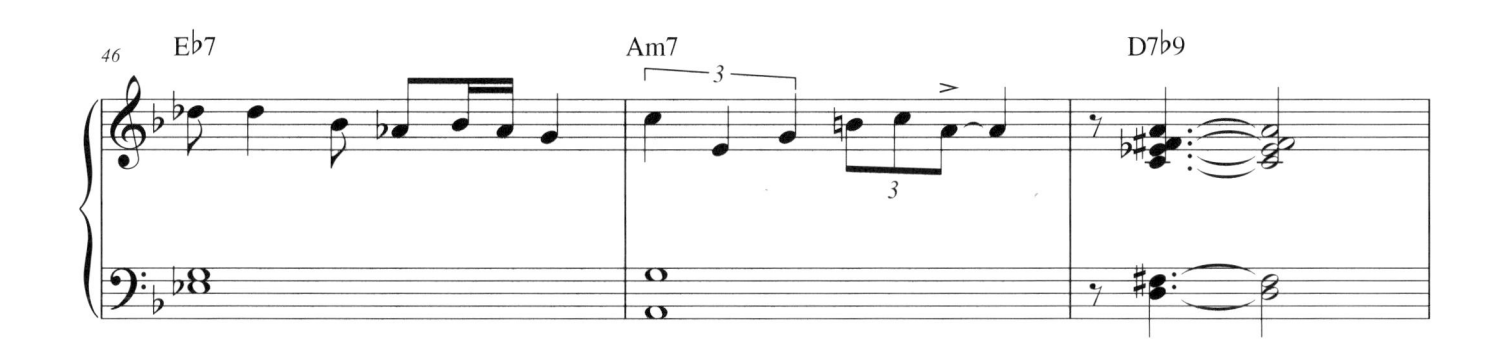

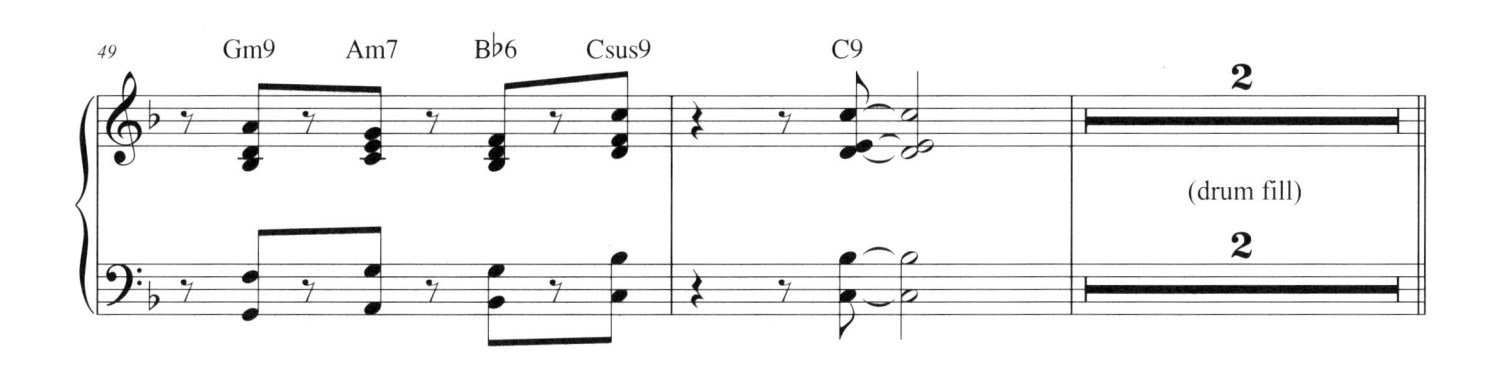

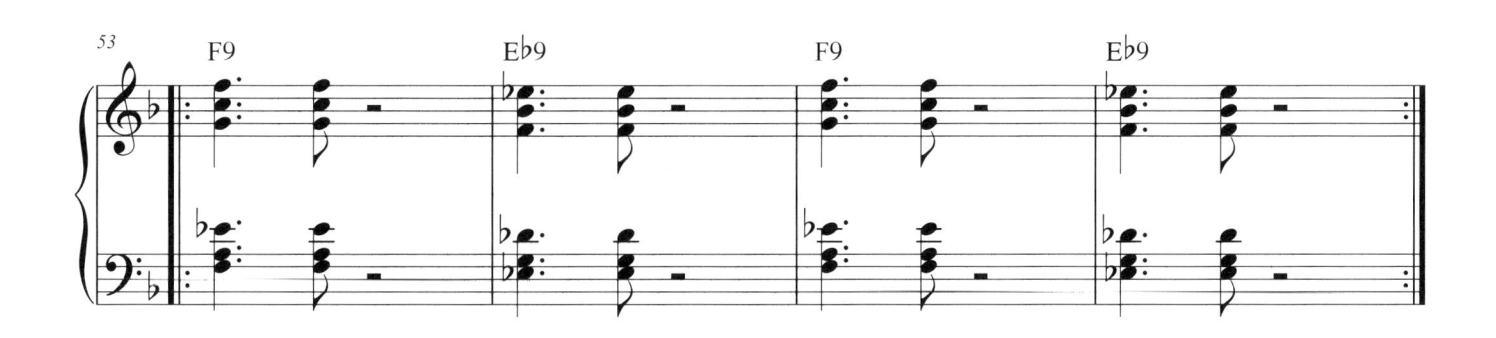

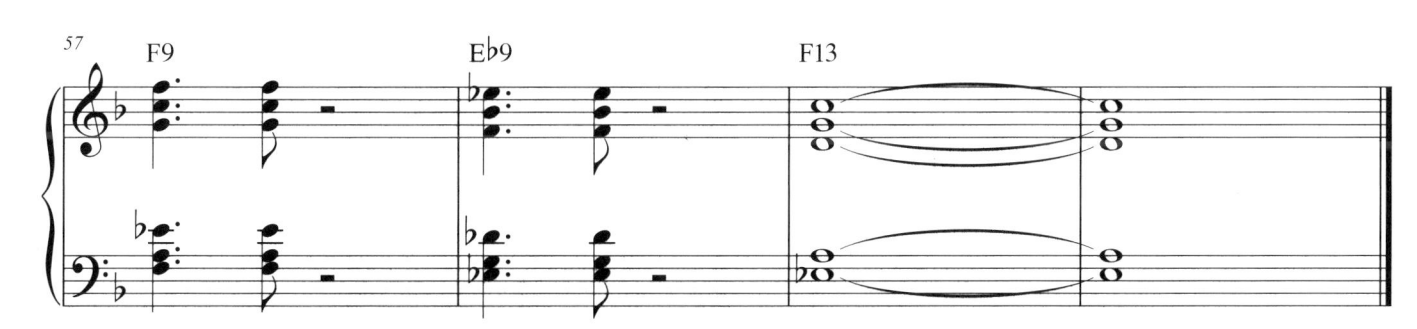

WEEKS 25-26
SALSA PIANO

Introduction to Salsa Jazz Piano

Salsa is a term used to describe Latin dance music found in Cuba and Puerto Rico. There are many styles that fall under the umbrella of Salsa: Rumba, Son, Danzon, Bolero, etc.

The Clave

Unlike Brazilian styles (bossa, samba, etc.), the study of Cuban music is based around a two-measure rhythmic pattern called "Clave." The main instrument that plays this pattern, by no coincidence, is named the clave. The clave pattern is organized in either 2-3 or 3-2 rhythmic cells. All other melodic and rhythmic ideas fit onto the foundation of these two clave patterns.

1. Son 2-3 Clave Pattern
   Clave
   Conga

2. Son 3-2 Clave Pattern
   Clave
   Conga

Below is a Son-Montuno pattern. This piano ostinato pattern is quite syncopated and deserves your attention. Please count carefully. Also, keep in mind that the clave part is heard mostly on the beat while your part is mostly on the off beats. This part is the basis for the Salsa Workout.

SALSA WORKOUT

This rhythm workout is most effective when practiced with the audio.

TRACK 13

Wayne Hawkins

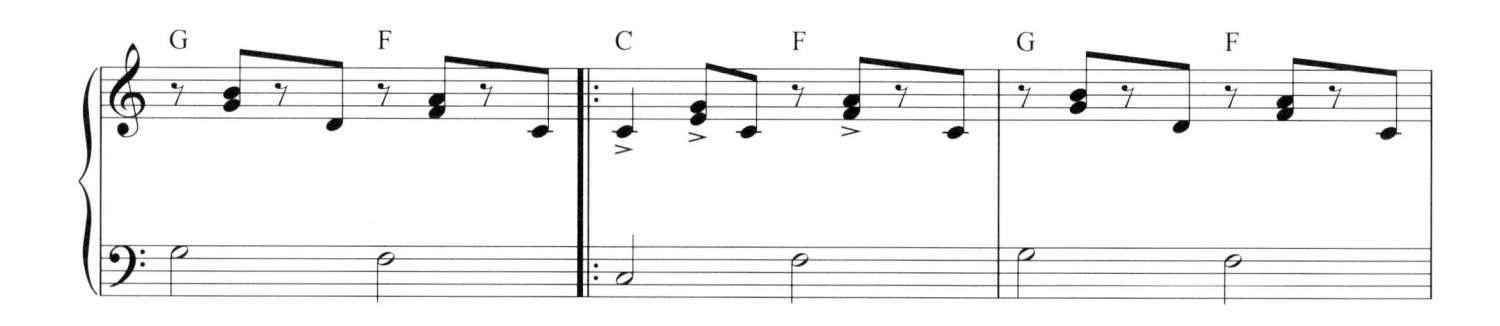

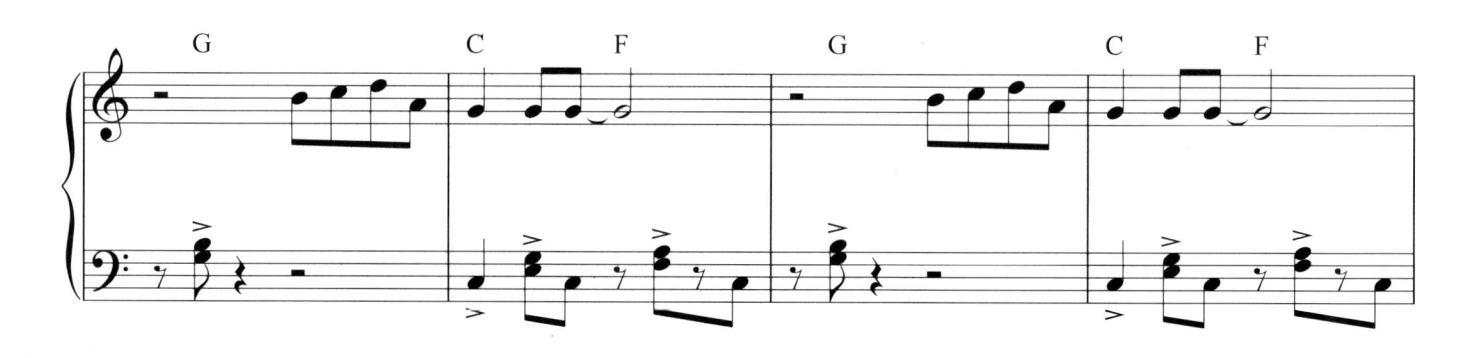

WEEKS 25-26

PIANO AEROBICS

45
C F G F C F
mf
cresc.
f
48
G F C F G F
C F G F C F
51
5 1 5 1 4 1 5 1
ff
54
G F C F G F
57
C F G C F G C

WEEKS 27-28
GOSPEL PIANO

The Backbeat

Gospel music has several things that are in common with most forms of popular music. For example, the backbeat is found in most rock, soul, and other popular forms. Often you will hear this played by the drummer on beats 2 and 4.

In gospel music, because of the different time signatures involved, the backbeat changes accordingly. Please study the following examples:

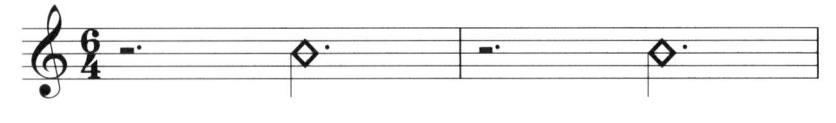

Harmonizing Scale Tones

One aspect of gospel music that has influenced many other styles is the harmonizing of scale tones. It makes a small idea sound big.

This is a three-note motive. It can also be the third, fourth, and fifth of a C scale, and if I choose to do so, I can harmonize it this way.

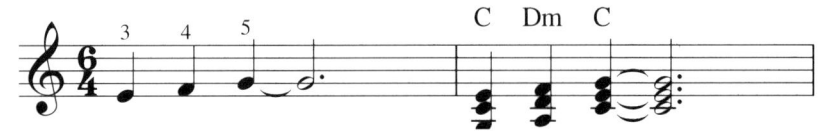

WEEKS 27-28

In playing the workout with the audio, please keep in mind that a saxophone player will be playing the melody with you, as well as improvising.

GOSPEL WORKOUT

Wayne Hawkins

TRACK 14

PIANO AEROBICS

35
39
43
3
47
51

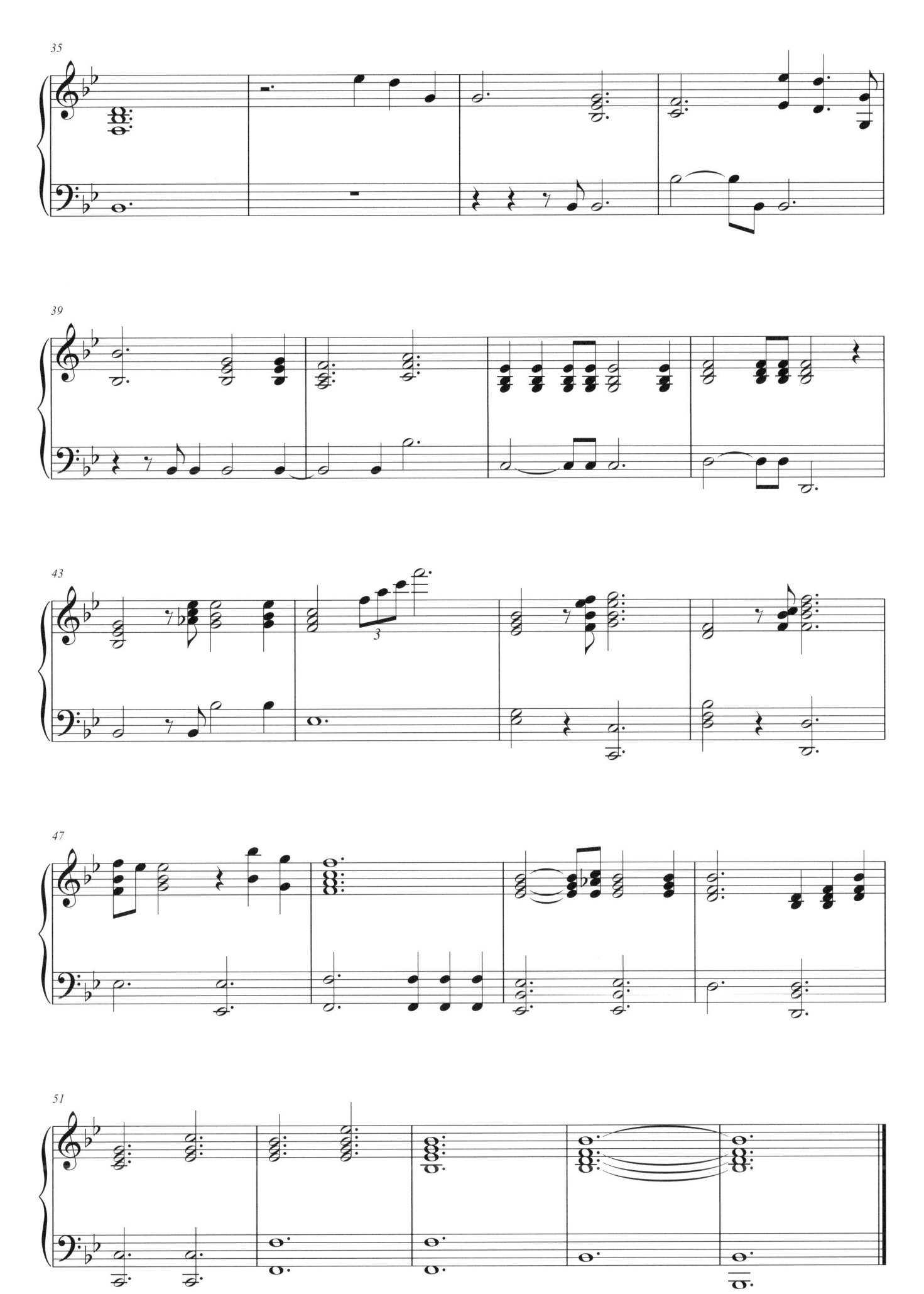

WEEKS 29-30

FOUR-HAND PIANO DUETS

Questions to Consider

In duets for four-hands, it is very important that both pianists ask themselves the following questions:

- What is the melody or foreground part?
- What is the function of my part?
- Could I possibly be playing either too loud or too soft?
- Could I be dragging or rushing?

In this workout, there is a special challenge. The left hand of Piano 1 (Primo) sometimes shares the same octave as the right hand of Piano 2 (Secondo). If each pianist plays in synchronization, moving the hand in and out at the correct time, no hands should crash.

PLEASE NOTE: Piano 1 (Primo) is on the right side and Piano 2 (Secondo) is on the left side. Students can use the accompanying audio to listen to the Primo and Secondo parts played together, or choose to play along with either the Secondo or Primo part separately. (Track 15: Primo and Secondo; Track 16: Secondo only; Track 17: Primo only.)

NEW AGE WORKOUT #2 (DUET)

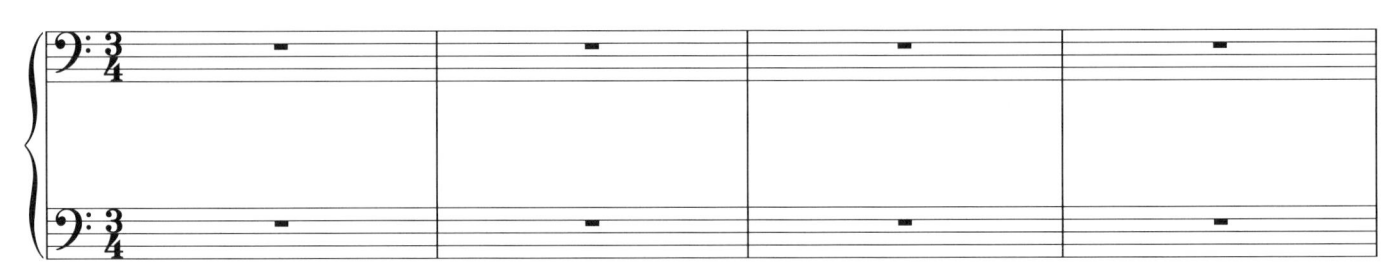

SECONDO

Wayne Hawkins

TRACKS 15-17

WEEKS 29-30

PRIMO

Wayne Hawkins

TRACKS 15-17

Smoothly, legato (♩ = 150)

ped. simile

poco a poco cresc.

PIANO AEROBICS

SECONDO

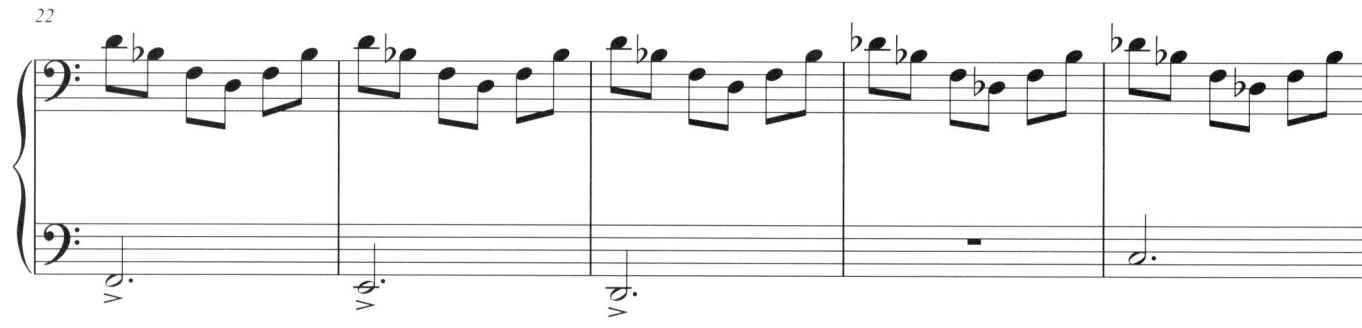

WEEKS 29-30

PRIMO

PIANO AEROBICS

SECONDO

WEEKS 29-30

PRIMO

WEEKS 31-32
JAZZ PIANO

Introduction to Swing and Bebop

Modern jazz piano has its roots in blues, stride, and swing styles. However, the modern era of jazz began with the development of bebop. From the bop era onward, jazz moved out of the popular music mainstream and into an art form. Some of the main points of change were:

1. Jazz developed a following of musicians and listeners alike who approach the music intellectually as well as emotionally.

2. To play jazz required a greater understanding of jazz theory and a higher level of virtuosity.

3. At first many bop tunes used form and harmony from existing 32 and 12-bar forms. Later on, more original, complicated forms and harmonies were introduced.

Jazz Exercises

Play this exercise, keeping in mind that all eighth-notes swing. In addition to swinging the eighth-notes, please play legato with slight accents as indicated.

This exercise follows the chord progression of the workout. All of the chords are on offbeats. Be sure to keep swinging the offbeats.

NOTE: In addition to providing a student with exposure to many of the styles of contemporary music, these workouts help to prepare a student to play with others. A jazz pianist will often play solo lines then accompany in a single chorus. When the pianist does this, it is in an even number of measures, most often in 4 measures. These measures will be marked as COMP and SOLO in the following workout.

MODERN JAZZ WORKOUT

Wayne Hawkins

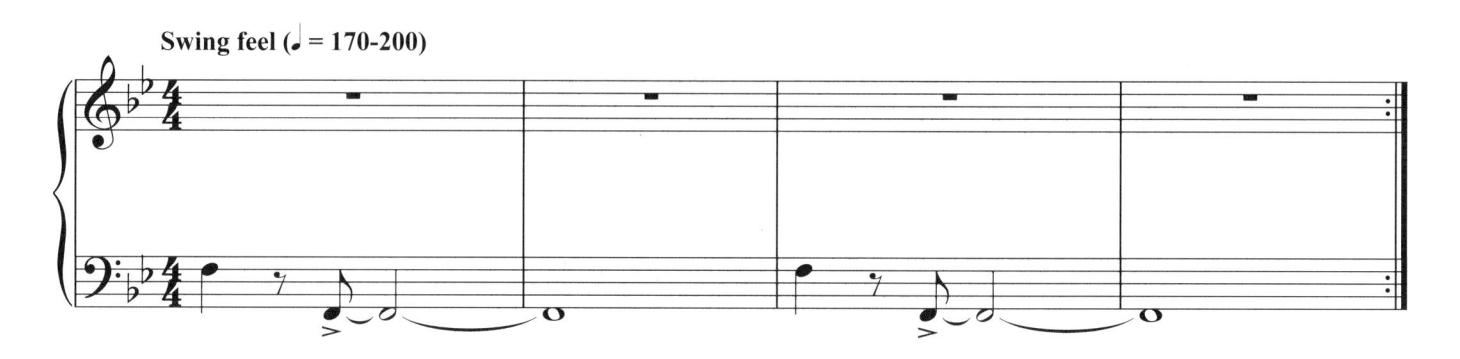

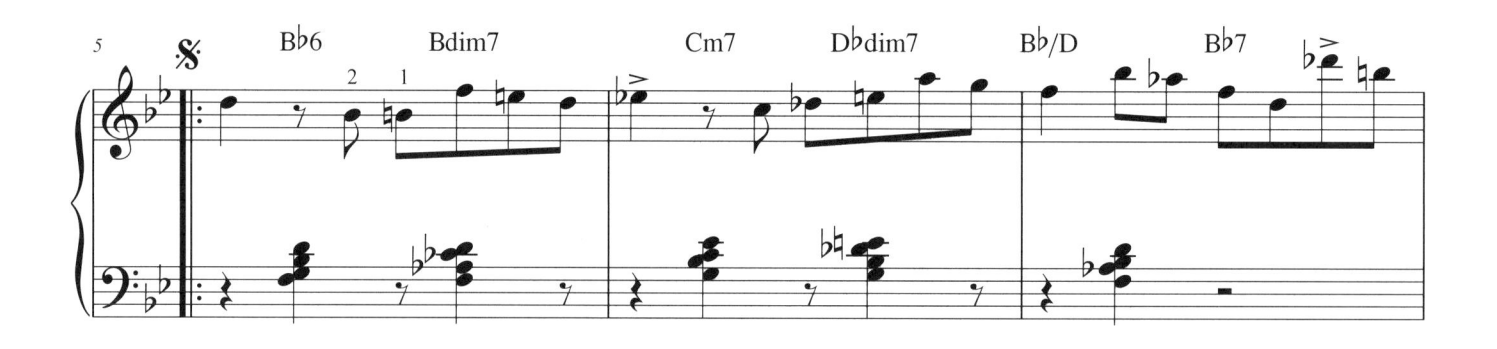

Swing feel (♩ = 170-200)

14
Cm9
F13♭9
B♭6
F7
17
D7♭9
G7♯11(♭9)
20
D♭7♯9
C7
C7♭9
23
F7♭9
B♭6
Bdim7

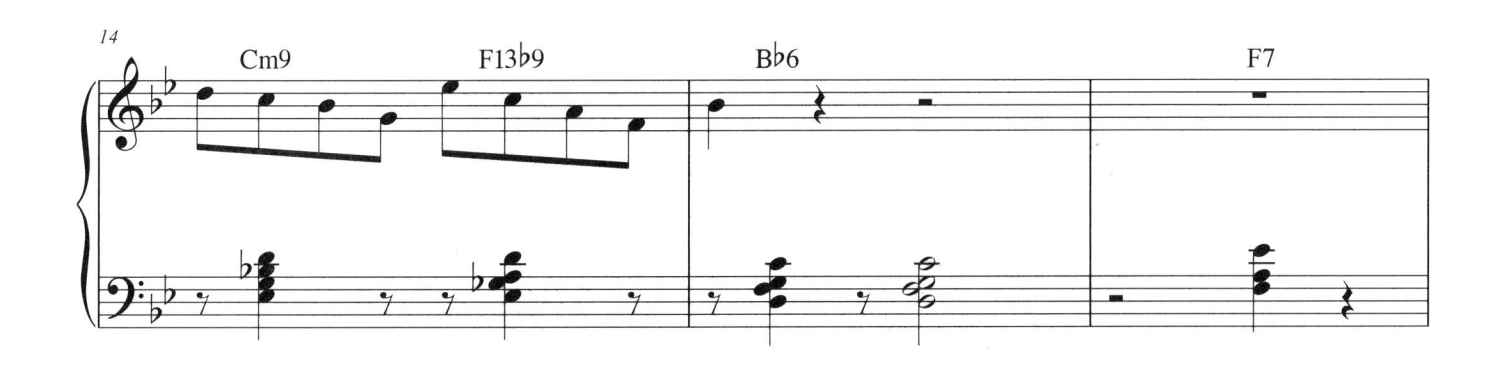

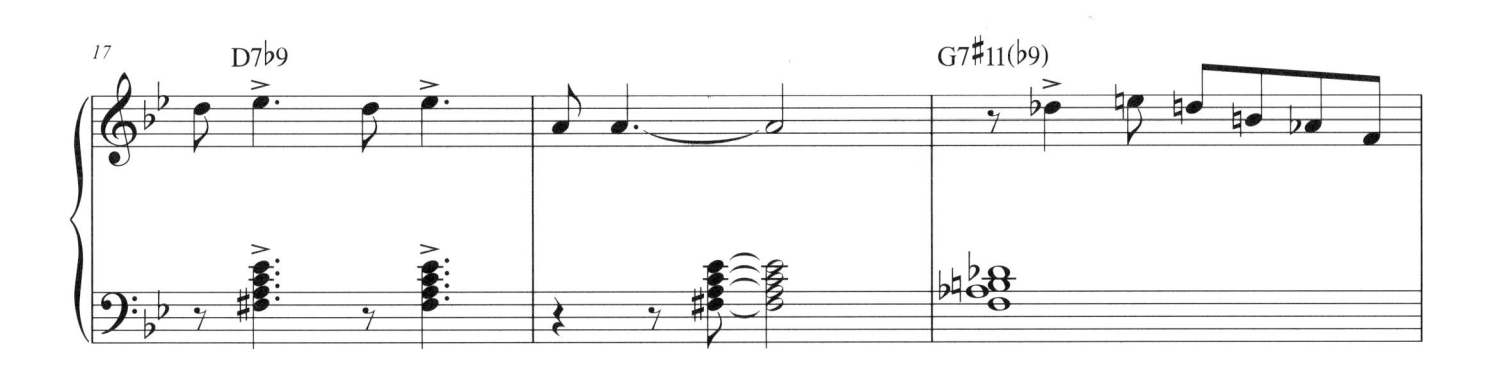

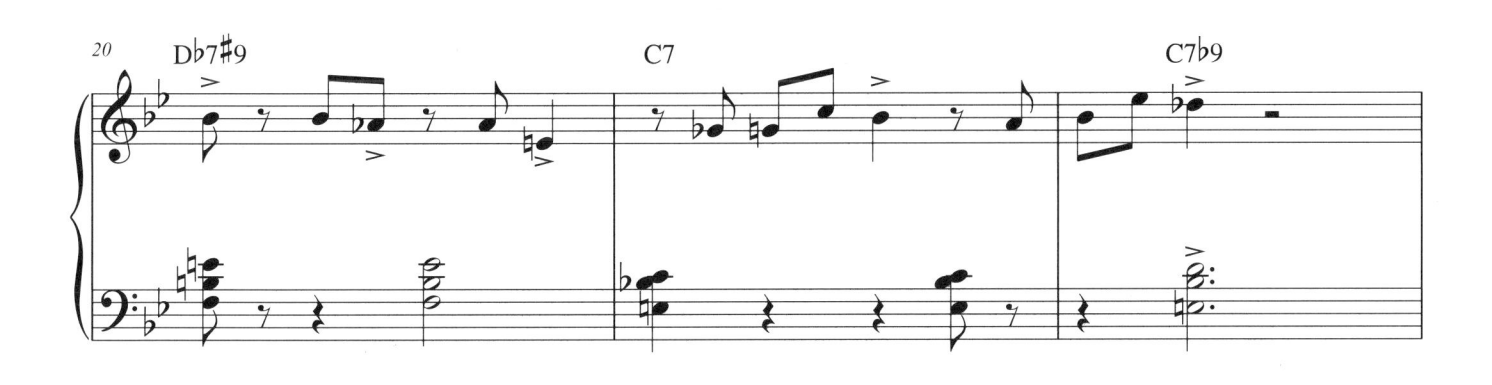

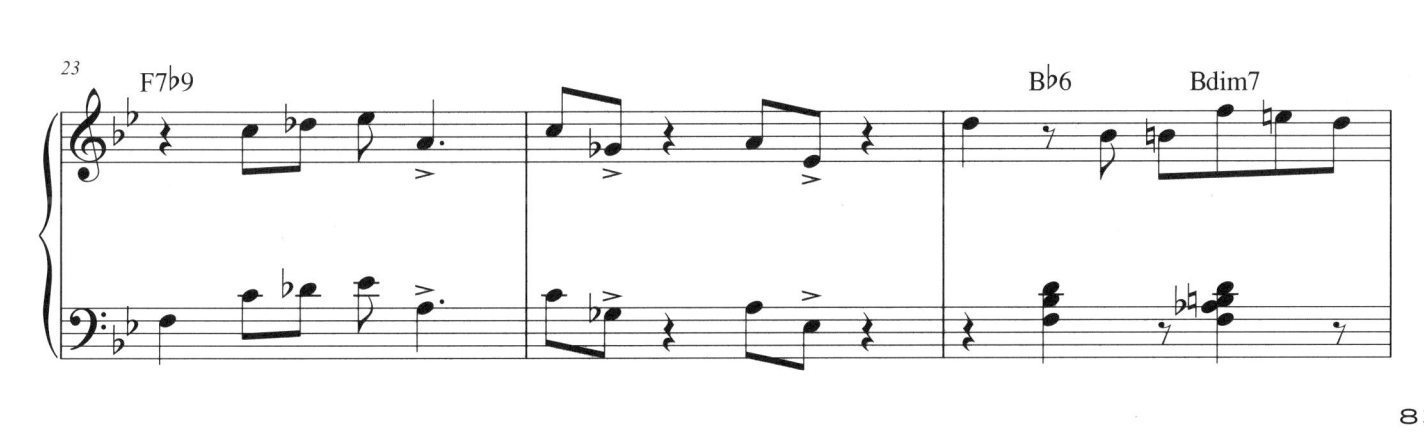

26
Cm7
D♭dim7
B♭/D
B♭7
E♭6
Edim7
29
B♭6/F
G7♭13
Cm9
F7
B♭6
Fine
COMP
33
B♭6
Bdim7
Cm7
D♭dim7
B♭6/D
B♭7
E♭6
Edim7
SOLO
37
B♭6
G7♭13
1 2 3 1 2 3 5
Cm7
F7
B♭6
F7♯9
COMP
41
B♭6
Bdim7
Cm9
D♭dim7
B♭6
B♭9
E♭6
Edim7

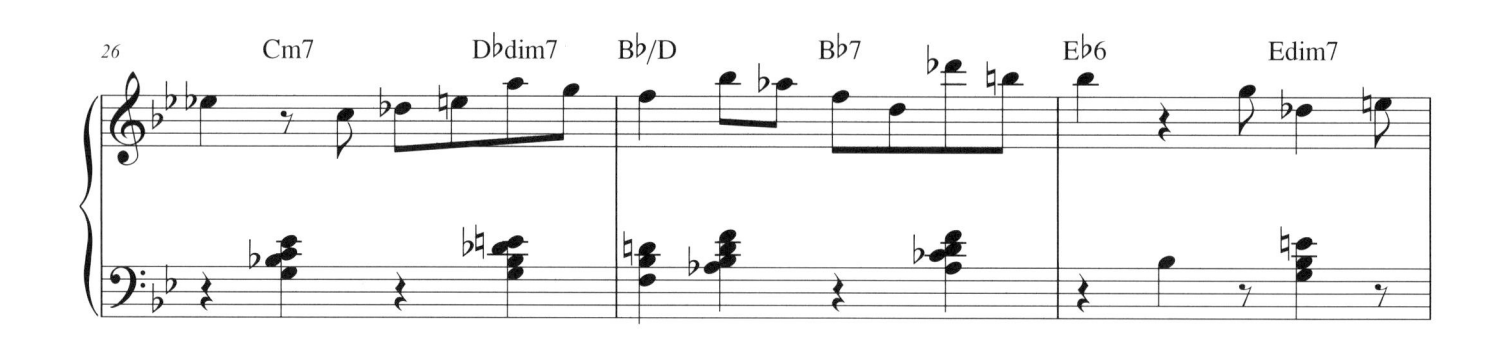

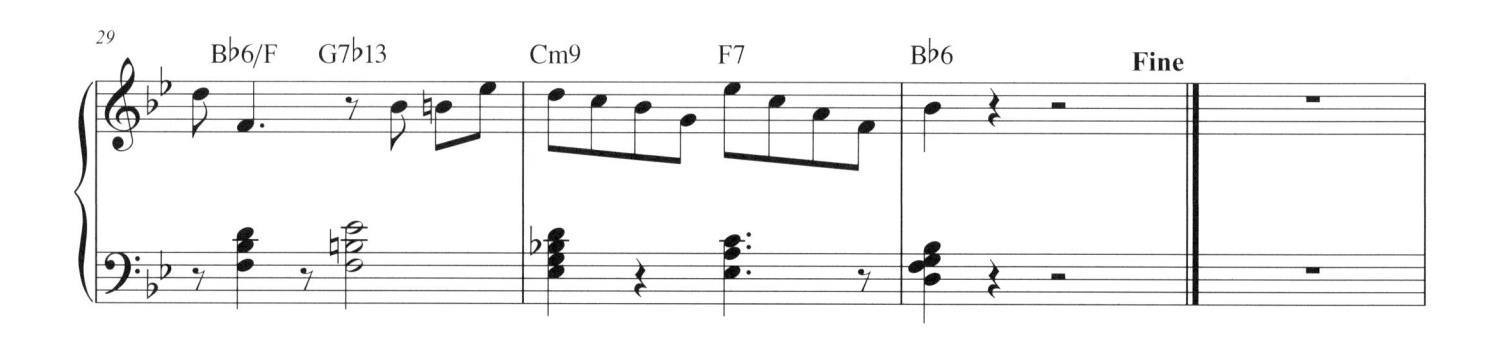

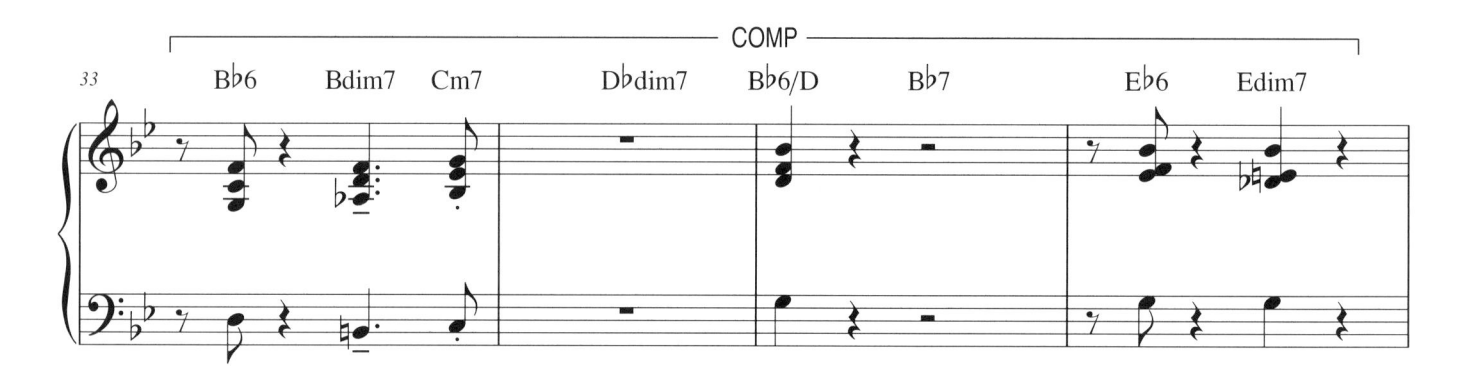

SOLO
45
Bb6/F G7/F Cm9 F7 Bb6 G7b13 F13
COMP
49
D7#9(b13) G13b9
SOLO
53
C7b9 F7b9
COMP
57
Bb6 Bdim7 Cm9 Dbdim7 Bb6/D Bb7 Eb6 Edim7
SOLO
61
Bb7/F G7b13 Cm9 F13b9 Bb6/F F9
D.S. al Fine
(with repeat)

WEEKS 33-34
EAR TRAINING

The Importance of Ear Training

The ability to listen to music as a musician rather than as a fan lies in ear training. Have you ever known anyone who could sit and play the piano without music and wished you could do the same? Have you ever heard something on the radio that you wished you could play? If so, this chapter will help you to make this happen. This section will have some notation, but the intent is for you to listen to the play along track and try to play what you hear.

Interval Training

Familiarize yourself with these intervals and try to remember their distinctive sound. There are seven interval examples in the workout. The soloist on the play-along track will play from the intervals listed in the exercise below. Please take a day with each interval. Practice with a partner playing the intervals for you.

Interval Exercises

Ear Training Workout

Unlike any of the previous workouts in this book, this workout has many options. The track will be approximately five minutes long. The sheet music of the workout has four different examples of rhythmic patterns and the student may play any of the four patterns. The track can also be used as an ear training exercise with the student listening and playing back exactly what the saxophone player plays. The saxophone will play one measure, then the student will imitate that measure in a call and response pattern.

EAR TRAINING WORKOUT
(Call and Response)

TRACK 19

Rhythm backgrounds (all on G7)

Pattern #1

Pattern #2

Pattern #3

Pattern #4

WEEKS 35-37
BRAZILIAN JAZZ

Brazilian Jazz Piano

Samba is one of the most famous styles of music from Brazil and became prominent in the 1930s. The *Choro* is one of the oldest styles of popular music, originating in the 1880s. Similar to the *Bossa Nova*, the *Samba* is a popular style used by jazz groups throughout the world. Larger ensembles were the first to feature this style.

Brazilian Jazz Exercises

There are two things that distinguish the Samba from other styles. The first is a non-syncopated rhythm, usually played by a bass (surdo) or lower drum (or sometimes the left hand of a pianist). The second is a syncopated rhythm often played by a little drum called the *tamborim* or the harmony instrument. Tap these rhythms below

You might notice that the exercises and workout are written in cut time. In both the Samba workout and the *Bossa Nova* workout, the music is felt in two. In fact, much of Brazilian music is written in 2/4. This workout is in 2/2 to make the rhythms easier to read.

You will be playing the figure below in the workout. Please tap this rhythm, then play the chords with a metronome set to ♩ = 90.

SAMBA WORKOUT

Wayne Hawkins

Lively (♩ = 90-100)

17
5
4
1
3
1
21
25
29
33
To Coda

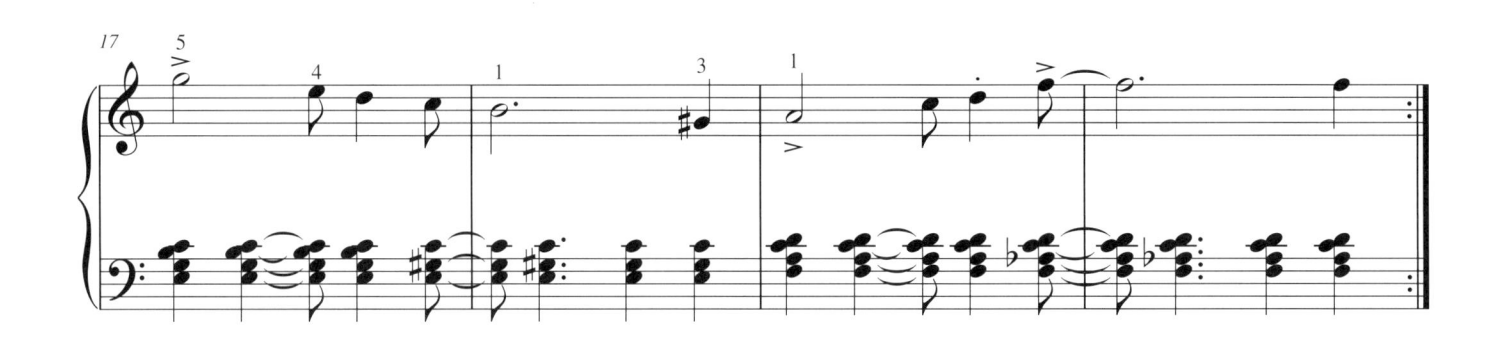

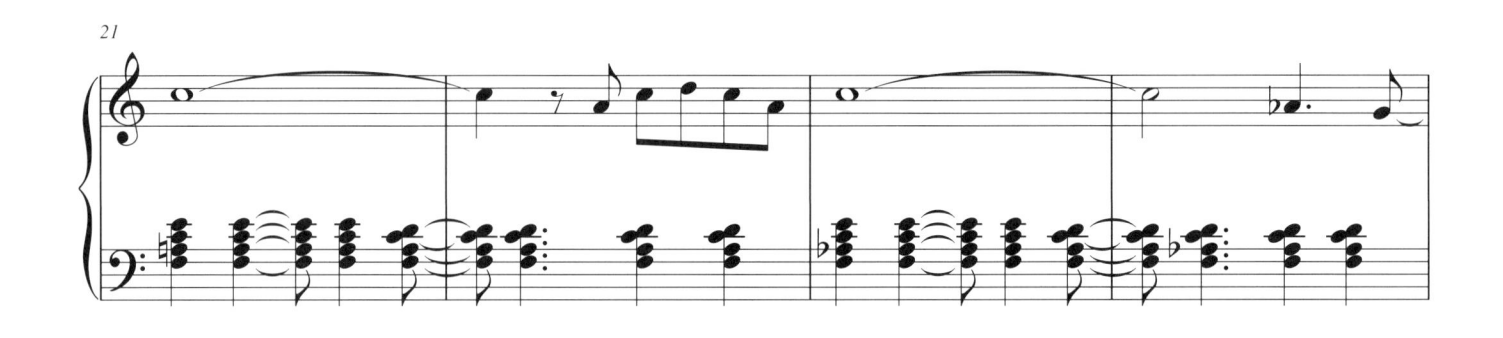

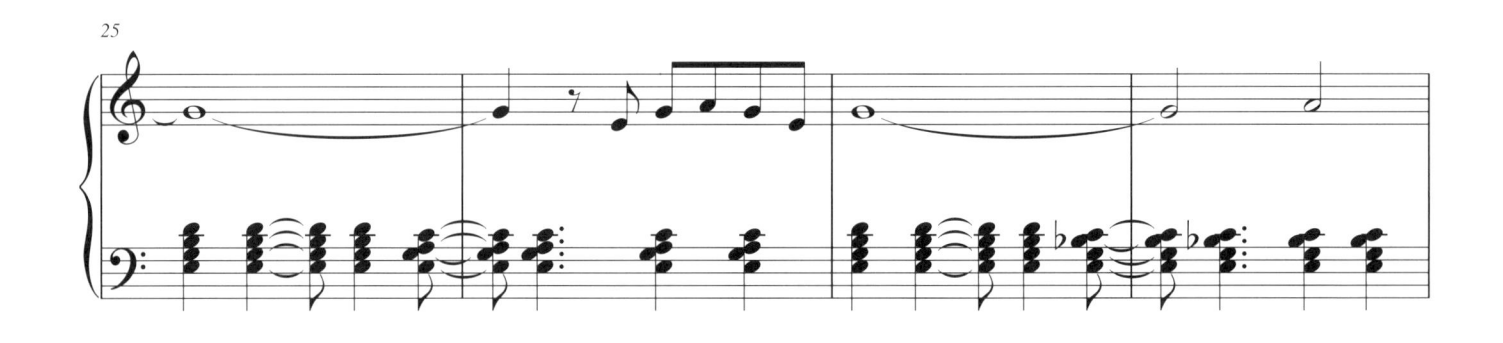

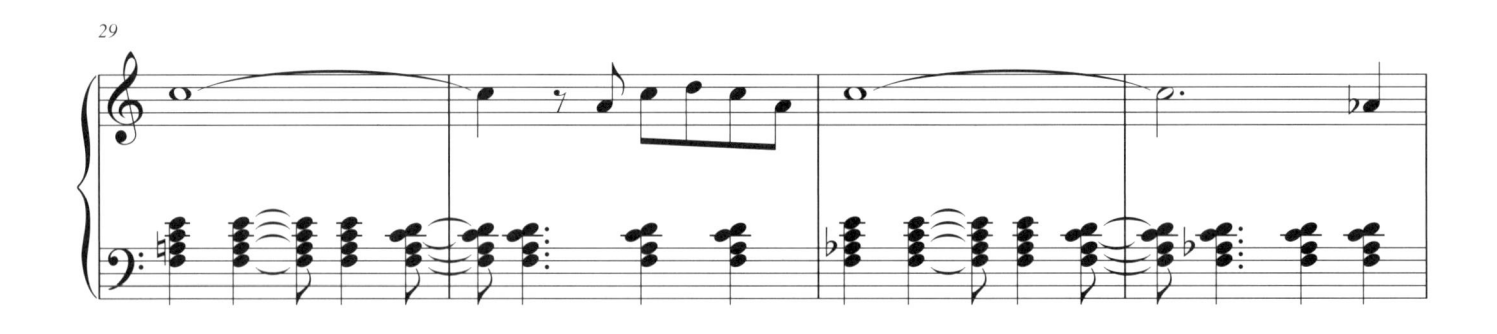

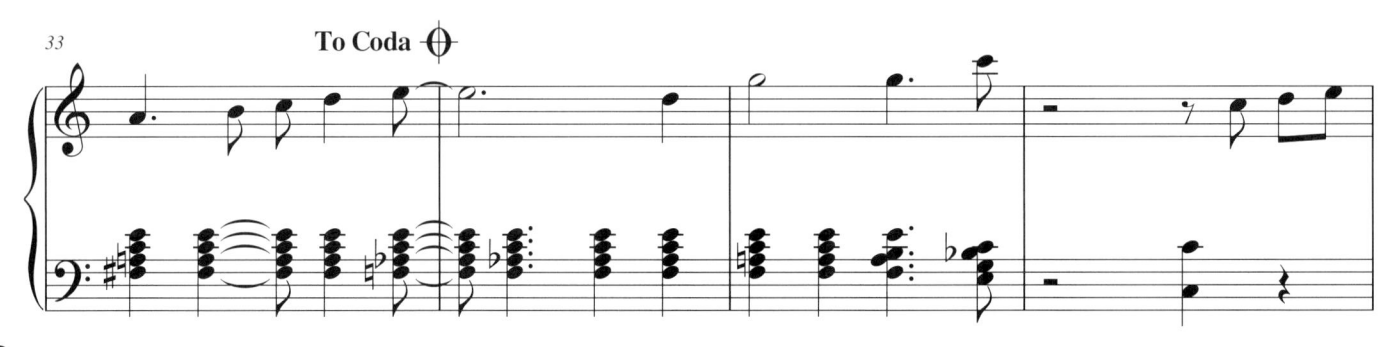

WEEKS 35-37

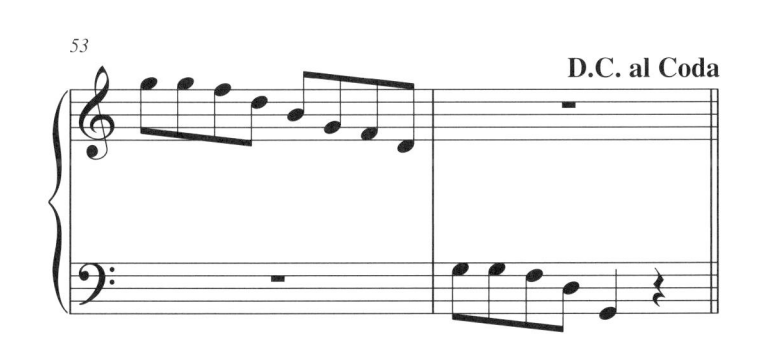

WEEKS 38-40
STRIDE PIANO

Use of the Left Hand in Ragtime and Jazz

Stride is a style of jazz piano that historically is a bridge between Ragtime and Swing styles. It thrived in the 1920s and 1930s. Stride features a more advanced use of the left hand as applied to Ragtime, while the right hand features swinging eighth-note rhythms.

Stride Exercises

Play the figure below without looking at your fingers. One key to playing with this technique is to move the hand early and to feel the keys with your fingertips.

This next figure is much more difficult. Play very slowly and increase the tempo gradually as you feel more comfortable.

When playing the workout, please keep in mind that the fingering given is for larger hands.

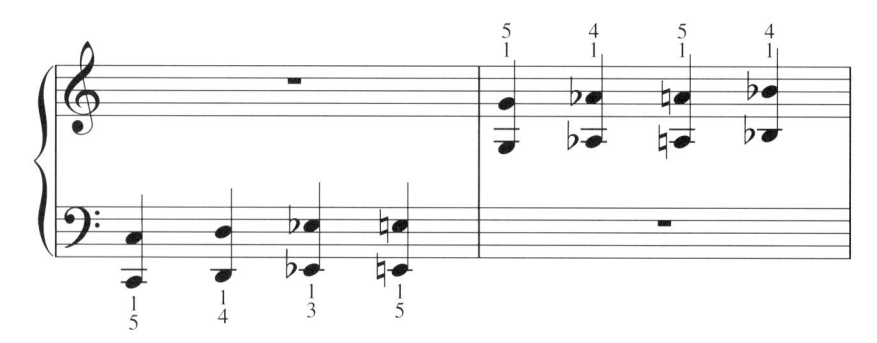

STRIDE WORKOUT

Wayne Hawkins

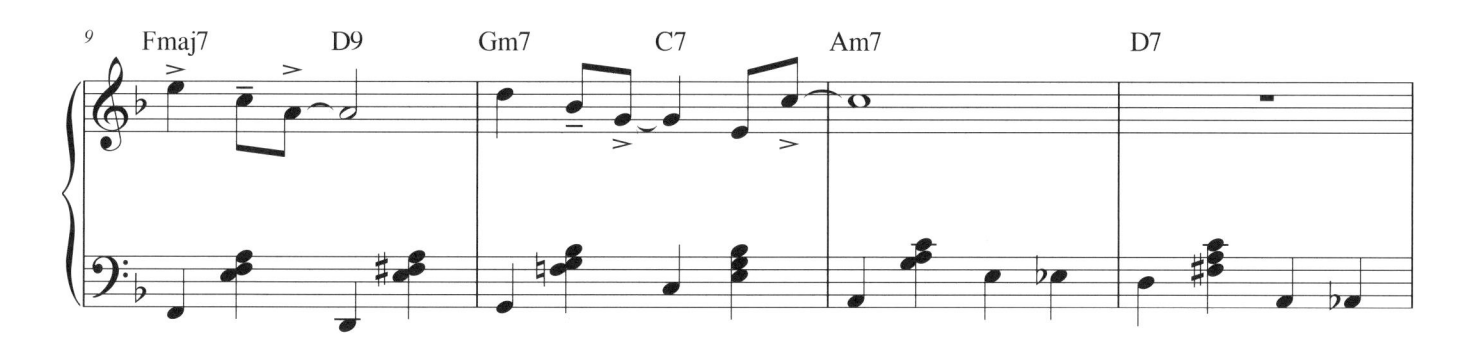

Swing feel (♩ = 120-150)

PIANO AEROBICS

WEEKS 38-40

KEYBOARD STYLE SERIES

THE COMPLETE GUIDE!

These book/audio packs provide focused lessons that contain valuable how-to insight, essential playing tips, and beneficial information for all players. From comping to soloing, comprehensive treatment is given to each subject. The companion audio features many of the examples in the book performed either solo or with a full band.

BEBOP JAZZ PIANO
by John Valerio
This book provides detailed information for bebop and jazz keyboardists on: chords and voicings, harmony and chord progressions, scales and tonality, common melodic figures and patterns, comping, characteristic tunes, the styles of Bud Powell and Thelonious Monk, and more.
00290535 Book/CD Pack..$18.99

BEGINNING ROCK KEYBOARD
by Mark Harrison
This comprehensive book/CD package will teach you the basic skills needed to play beginning rock keyboard. From comping to soloing, you'll learn the theory, the tools, and the techniques used by the pros. The accompanying CD demonstrates most of the music examples in the book.
00311922 Book/CD Pack..$14.99

BLUES PIANO
by Mark Harrison
With this book/audio pack, you'll learn the theory, the tools, and even the tricks that the pros use to play the blues. Covers: scales and chords; left-hand patterns; walking bass; endings and turnarounds; right-hand techniques; how to solo with blues scales; crossover licks; and more.
00311007 Book/Online Audio $17.99

BOOGIE-WOOGIE PIANO
by Todd Lowry
From learning the basic chord progressions to inventing your own melodic riffs, you'll learn the theory, tools and techniques used by the genre's best practitioners.
00117067 Book/Online Audio $17.99

BRAZILIAN PIANO
by Robert Willey and Alfredo Cardim
Brazilian Piano teaches elements of some of the most appealing Brazilian musical styles: choro, samba, and bossa nova. It starts with rhythmic training to develop the fundamental groove of Brazilian music.
00311469 Book/Online Audio $19.99

CONTEMPORARY JAZZ PIANO
by Mark Harrison
From comping to soloing, you'll learn the theory, the tools, and the techniques used by the pros. The full band tracks on the CD feature the rhythm section on the left channel and the piano on the right channel, so that you can play along with the band.
00311848 Book/CD Pack..$17.99

COUNTRY PIANO
by Mark Harrison
Learn the theory, the tools, and the tricks used by the pros to get that authentic country sound. This book/audio pack covers: scales and chords, walkup and walkdown patterns, comping in traditional and modern country, Nashville "fretted piano" techniques and more.
00311052 Book/Online Audio $19.99

GOSPEL PIANO
by Kurt Cowling
Discover the tools you need to play in a variety of authentic gospel styles, through a study of rhythmic devices, grooves, melodic and harmonic techniques, and formal design. The accompanying audio features over 90 tracks, including piano examples as well as the full gospel band.
00311327 Book/Online Adio $17.99

INTRO TO JAZZ PIANO
by Mark Harrison
From comping to soloing, you'll learn the theory, the tools, and the techniques used by the pros. The accompanying audio demonstrates most of the music examples in the book. The full band tracks feature the rhythm section on the left channel and the piano on the right channel, so that you can play along with the band.
00312088 Book/Online Audio $16.99

JAZZ-BLUES PIANO
by Mark Harrison
This comprehensive book will teach you the basic skills needed to play jazz-blues piano. Topics covered include: scales and chords • harmony and voicings • progressions and comping • melodies and soloing • characteristic stylings.
00311243 Book/Online Audio $17.99

JAZZ-ROCK KEYBOARD
by T. Lavitz
Learn what goes into mixing the power and drive of rock music with the artistic elements of jazz improvisation in this comprehensive book and CD package. This instructional tool delves into scales and modes, and how they can be used with various chord progressions to develop the best in soloing chops.
00290536 Book/CD Pack..$17.95

LATIN JAZZ PIANO
by John Valerio
This book is divided into three sections. The first covers Afro-Cuban (Afro-Caribbean) jazz, the second section deals with Brazilian influenced jazz – Bossa Nova and Samba, and the third contains lead sheets of the tunes and instructions for the play-along CD.
00311345 Book/CD Pack..$17.99

MODERN POP KEYBOARD
by Mark Harrison
From chordal comping to arpeggios and ostinatos, from grand piano to synth pads, you'll learn the theory, the tools, and the techniques used by the pros. The online audio demonstrates most of the music examples in the book.
00146596 Book/Online Audio $17.99

NEW AGE PIANO
by Todd Lowry
From melodic development to chord progressions to left-hand accompaniment patterns, you'll learn the theory, the tools and the techniques used by the pros. The accompanying 96-track CD demonstrates most of the music examples in the book.
00117322 Book/CD Pack..$16.99

POST-BOP JAZZ PIANO
by John Valerio
This book/audio pack will teach you the basic skills needed to play post-bop jazz piano. Learn the theory, the tools, and the tricks used by the pros to play in the style of Bill Evans, Thelonious Monk, Herbie Hancock, McCoy Tyner, Chick Corea and others. Topics covered include: chord voicings, scales and tonality, modality, and more.
00311005 Book/Online Audio $17.99

PROGRESSIVE ROCK KEYBOARD
by Dan Maske
You'll learn how soloing techniques, form, rhythmic and metrical devices, harmony, and counterpoint all come together to make this style of rock the unique and exciting genre it is.
00311307 Book/CD Pack..$17.95

R&B KEYBOARD
by Mark Harrison
From soul to funk to disco to pop, you'll learn the theory, the tools, and the tricks used by the pros with this book/audio pack. Topics covered include: scales and chords, harmony and voicings, progressions and comping, rhythmic concepts, characteristic stylings, the development of R&B, and more! Includes seven songs.
00310881 Book/Online Audio $19.99

ROCK KEYBOARD
by Scott Miller
Learn to comp or solo in any of your favorite rock styles. Listen to the audio to hear your parts fit in with the total groove of the band. Includes 99 tracks! Covers: classic rock, pop/rock, blues rock, Southern rock, hard rock, progressive rock, alternative rock and heavy metal.
00310823 Book/Online Audio $17.95

ROCK 'N' ROLL PIANO
by Andy Vinter
Take your place alongside Fats Domino, Jerry Lee Lewis, Little Richard, and other legendary players of the '50s and '60s! This book/audio pack covers: left-hand patterns; basic rock 'n' roll progressions; right-hand techniques; straight eighths vs. swing eighths; glisses, crushed notes, rolls, note clusters and more. Includes six complete tunes.
00310912 Book/Online Audio $17.99

SALSA PIANO
by Hector Martignon
From traditional Cuban music to the more modern Puerto Rican and New York styles, you'll learn the all-important rhythmic patterns of salsa and how to apply them to the piano. The book provides historical, geographical and cultural background info, and the 50+-tracks includes piano examples and a full salsa band percussion section.
00311049 Book/Online Audio $19.99

SMOOTH JAZZ PIANO
by Mark Harrison
Learn the skills you need to play smooth jazz piano – the theory, the tools, and the tricks used by the pros. Topics covered include: scales and chords; harmony and voicings; progressions and comping; rhythmic concepts; melodies and soloing; characteristic stylings; discussions on jazz evolution.
00311095 Book/Online Audio $17.99

STRIDE & SWING PIANO
by John Valerio
Learn the styles of the stride and swing piano masters, such as Scott Joplin, Jimmy Yancey, Pete Johnson, Jelly Roll Morton, James P. Johnson, Fats Waller, Teddy Wilson, and Art Tatum. This book/audio pack covers classic ragtime, early blues and boogie woogie, New Orleans jazz and more. Includes 14 songs.
00310882 Book/Online Audio $19.99

HAL•LEONARD®

Prices, contents, and availability subject to change without notice.

www.halleonard.com

HAL•LEONARD KEYBOARD PLAY-ALONG

The **Keyboard Play-Along** series will help you quickly and easily play your favorite songs as played by your favorite artists. Just follow the music in the book, listen to the CD or online audio to hear how the keyboard should sound, and then play along using the separate backing tracks. The melody and lyrics are also included in the book in case you want to sing, or simply to help you follow along. The audio CD is playable on any CD player. For PC and Mac users, the CD is enhanced so you can adjust the recording to any tempo without changing pitch! Each book/audio pack in this series features eight great songs.

1. POP/ROCK HITS
Against All Odds (Take a Look at Me Now) • Deacon Blues • (Everything I Do) I Do It for You • Hard to Say I'm Sorry • Kiss on My List • My Life • Walking in Memphis • What a Fool Believes.
00699875 Keyboard Transcriptions $14.95

2. SOFT ROCK
Don't Know Much • Glory of Love • I Write the Songs • It's Too Late • Just Once • Making Love Out of Nothing at All • We've Only Just Begun • You Are the Sunshine of My Life.
00699876 Keyboard Transcriptions $14.95

3. CLASSIC ROCK
Against the Wind • Come Sail Away • Don't Do Me like That • Jessica • Say You Love Me • Takin' Care of Business • Werewolves of London • You're My Best Friend.
00699877 Keyboard Transcriptions $14.95

5. ROCK HITS
Back at One • Brick • Clocks • Drops of Jupiter (Tell Me) • Home • 100 Years • This Love • You're Beautiful
00699879 Keyboard Transcriptions $14.95

6. ROCK BALLADS
Bridge over Troubled Water • Easy • Hey Jude • Imagine • Maybe I'm Amazed • A Whiter Shade of Pale • You Are So Beautiful • Your Song.
00699880 Keyboard Transcriptions $14.95

7. ROCK CLASSICS
Baba O'Riley • Bloody Well Right • Carry on Wayward Son • Changes • Cold As Ice • Evil Woman • Space Truckin' • That's All.
00699881 Keyboard Transcriptions $14.95

8. BILLY JOEL – CLASSICS
Angry Young Man • Captain Jack • Honesty • Movin' Out (Anthony's Song) • My Life • Only the Good Die Young • Piano Man • Summer, Highland Falls.
00700302 Keyboard Transcriptions $14.99

9. ELTON JOHN BALLADS
Blue Eyes • Candle in the Wind • Daniel • Don't Let the Sun Go Down on Me • Goodbye Yellow Brick Road • Rocket Man (I Think It's Gonna Be a Long Long Time) • Someone Saved My Life Tonight • Sorry Seems to Be the Hardest Word.
00700752 Keyboard Transcriptions $14.99

10. STEELY DAN
Aja • Do It Again • FM • Hey Nineteen • Peg • Reeling in the Years • Rikki Don't Lose That Number.
00700201 Keyboard Transcriptions $14.99

12. CHRISTMAS HITS
Baby, It's Cold Outside • Blue Christmas • Merry Christmas, Darling • Mistletoe and Wine • Santa Baby • A Spaceman Came Travelling • Step into Christmas • Wonderful Christmastime.
00700267 Keyboard Transcriptions $14.95

13. BILLY JOEL – HITS
Allentown • Just the Way You Are • New York State of Mind • Pressure • Root Beer Rag • Scenes from an Italian Restaurant • She's Always a Woman • Tell Her About It.
00700303 Keyboard Transcriptions $14.99

14. LENNON & McCARTNEY
All You Need Is Love • Back in the U.S.S.R. • Come Together • Get Back • Good Day Sunshine • Hey Jude • Penny Lane • Revolution.
00700754 Keyboard Transcriptions $14.99

15. ELVIS PRESLEY
All Shook Up • A Big Hunk O' Love • Blue Suede Shoes • Can't Help Falling in Love • Don't Be Cruel (To a Heart That's True) • I Want You, I Need You, I Love You • Jailhouse Rock • Love Me.
00700755 Keyboard Transcriptions $14.99

16. 1970s ROCK
Dream On • Highway Star • I Feel the Earth Move • Foreplay/Long Time (Long Time) • Point of Know Return • Sweet Home Alabama • Take the Long Way Home • Will It Go Round in Circles.
00700933 Keyboard Transcriptions $14.99

17. 1960s ROCK
Gimme Some Lovin' • Green Onions • I'm a Believer • Louie, Louie • Magic Carpet Ride • Oh, Pretty Woman • Runaway • The Twist.
00700935 Keyboard Transcriptions $14.99

18. 1950s ROCK
Blueberry Hill • Good Golly Miss Molly • Great Balls of Fire • The Great Pretender • Rock and Roll Is Here to Stay • Shake, Rattle and Roll • Tutti Frutti • What'd I Say.
00700934 Keyboard Transcriptions $14.99

19. JAZZ CLASSICS
Blues Etude • (They Long to Be) Close to You • Freeway • Lonely Woman • My Foolish Heart • Tin Tin Deo • Watch What Happens.
00701244 Keyboard Transcriptions $14.99

20. STEVIE WONDER
Boogie On Reggae Woman • Higher Ground • I Wish • Isn't She Lovely • Living for the City • Sir Duke • Superstition • You Are the Sunshine of My Life.
00701262 Keyboard Transcriptions $14.99

21. R&B
Baby Love • Easy • For Once in My Life • I Can't Help Myself (Sugar Pie, Honey Bunch) • I Heard It Through the Grapevine • Mess Around • Respect • Respect Yourself.
00701263 Keyboard Transcriptions $14.99

22. CAROLE KING
I Feel the Earth Move • It's Too Late • Jazzman • (You Make Me Feel Like) a Natural Woman • So Far Away • Sweet Seasons • Will You Love Me Tomorrow (Will You Still Love Me Tomorrow) • You've Got a Friend.
00701756 Keyboard Transcriptions $14.99

HAL•LEONARD® CORPORATION
7777 W. BLUEMOUND RD. P.O. BOX 13819
MILWAUKEE, WISCONSIN 53213
www.halleonard.com

Prices, contents, and availability subject to change without notice.

THE ULTIMATE SONGBOOKS

Hal Leonard Piano Play-Along

These great songbooks come with our standard arrangements for piano and voice with guitar chord frames plus audio.

Each book includes either a CD or access to online recordings of full performance of each song, as well as a second track without the piano part so you can play "lead" with the band!

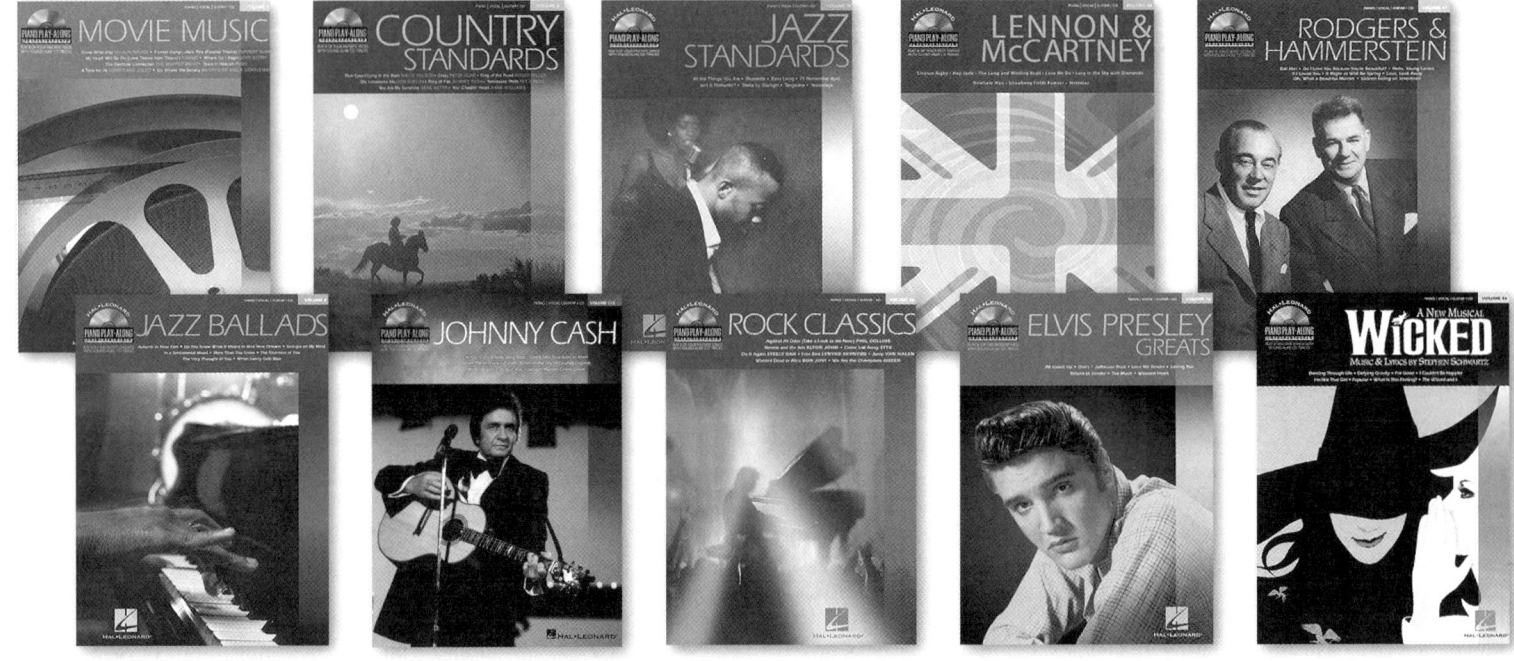

1. MOVIE MUSIC
00311072 P/V/G $14.95

2. JAZZ BALLADS
00311073 P/V/G $14.95

4. BROADWAY CLASSICS
00311075 P/V/G $14.95

5. DISNEY
00311076 P/V/G $14.95

6. COUNTRY STANDARDS
00311077 P/V/G $14.99

7. LOVE SONGS
00311078 P/V/G $14.95

9. CHILDREN'S SONGS
0311080 P/V/G $14.95

10. WEDDING CLASSICS
00311081 Piano Solo $14.95

11. WEDDING FAVORITES
00311097 P/V/G $14.95

12. CHRISTMAS FAVORITES
00311137 P/V/G $15.95

13. YULETIDE FAVORITES
00311138 P/V/G $14.95

14. POP BALLADS
00311145 P/V/G $14.95

15. FAVORITE STANDARDS
00311146 P/V/G $14.95

17. MOVIE FAVORITES
00311148 P/V/G $14.95

18. JAZZ STANDARDS
00311149 P/V/G $14.95

19. CONTEMPORARY HITS
00311162 P/V/G $14.95

20. R&B BALLADS
00311163 P/V/G $14.95

21. BIG BAND
00311164 P/V/G $14.95

22. ROCK CLASSICS
00311165 P/V/G $14.95

23. WORSHIP CLASSICS
00311166 P/V/G $14.95

24. LES MISÉRABLES
00311169 P/V/G $14.95

25. THE SOUND OF MUSIC
00311175 P/V/G $15.99

28. LENNON & MCCARTNEY
00311180 P/V/G $14.95

29. THE BEACH BOYS
00311181 P/V/G $14.95

30. ELTON JOHN
00311182 P/V/G $14.95

31. CARPENTERS
00311183 P/V/G $14.95

33. PEANUTS™
00311227 P/V/G $14.95

34 CHARLIE BROWN CHRISTMAS
00311228 P/V/G $15.95

35. ELVIS PRESLEY HITS
00311230 P/V/G $14.95

36. ELVIS PRESLEY GREATS
00311231 P/V/G $14.95

44. FRANK SINATRA – POPULAR HITS
00311277 P/V/G $14.95

45. FRANK SINATRA – MOST REQUESTED SONGS
00311278 P/V/G $14.95

46. WICKED
00311317 P/V/G $16.99

47. RENT
00311319 P/V/G $14.95

48. CHRISTMAS CAROLS
00311332 P/V/G $14.95

49. HOLIDAY HITS
00311333 P/V/G $15.99

50. DISNEY CLASSICS
00311417 P/V/G $14.95

53. GREASE
00311450 P/V/G $14.95

56. THE 1950S
00311459 P/V/G $14.95

61. BILLY JOEL FAVORITES
00311464 P/V/G $14.95

62. BILLY JOEL HITS
00311465 P/V/G $14.95

63. MAROON 5
00316826 P/V/G $14.99

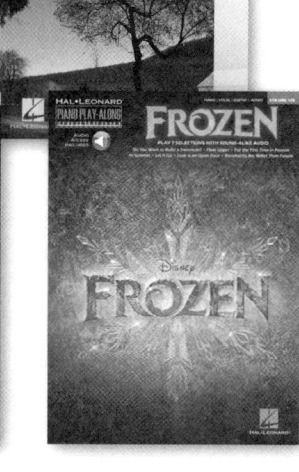

64. GOD BLESS AMERICA
00311489 P/V/G $14.95

65. CASTING CROWNS
00311494 P/V/G $14.95

68. LENNON & McCARTNEY FAVORITES
00311804 P/V/G $14.99

69. PIRATES OF THE CARIBBEAN
00311807 P/V/G $15.99

71. GEORGE GERSHWIN
00102687 P/V/G $24.99

72. VAN MORRISON
00103053 P/V/G $14.99

73. MAMMA MIA! – THE MOVIE
00311831 P/V/G $15.99

74. COLE PORTER
00311844 P/V/G $14.99

75. TWILIGHT
00311860 P/V/G $16.99

76. PRIDE & PREJUDICE
00311862 P/V/G $14.99

77. ELTON JOHN FAVORITES
00311884 P/V/G $14.99

78. ERIC CLAPTON
00311885 P/V/G $14.99

79. TANGOS
00311886 P/V/G $14.99

80. FIDDLER ON THE ROOF
00311887 P/V/G $14.99

81. JOSH GROBAN
00311901 P/V/G $14.99

82. LIONEL RICHIE
00311902 P/V/G $14.99

83. PHANTOM OF THE OPERA
00311903 P/V/G $15.99

84. ANTONIO CARLOS JOBIM FAVORITES
00311919 P/V/G $14.99

85. LATIN FAVORITES
00311920 P/V/G $14.99

86. BARRY MANILOW
00311935 P/V/G $14.99

87. PATSY CLINE
00311936 P/V/G $14.99

88. NEIL DIAMOND
00311937 P/V/G $14.99

89. FAVORITE HYMNS
00311940 P/V/G $14.99

90. IRISH FAVORITES
00311969 P/V/G $14.99

92. DISNEY FAVORITES
00311973 P/V/G $14.99

93. THE TWILIGHT SAGA: NEW MOON – SOUNDTRACK
00311974 P/V/G $16.99

94. THE TWILIGHT SAGA: NEW MOON – SCORE
00311975 P/V/G $16.99

95. TAYLOR SWIFT
00311984 P/V/G $14.99

96. BEST OF LENNON & McCARTNEY
00311996 P/V/G $14.99

97. GREAT CLASSICAL THEMES
00312020 PIANO SOLO $14.99

98. CHRISTMAS CHEER
00312021 P/V/G $14.99

99. ANTONIO CARLOS JOBIM CLASSICS
00312039 P/V/G $14.99

100. COUNTRY CLASSICS
00312041 P/V/G $14.99

102. GLEE
00312043 P/V/G $15.99

103. GOSPEL FAVORITES
00312044 P/V/G $14.99

105. BEE GEES
00312055 P/V/G $14.99

106. CAROLE KING
00312056 P/V/G $14.99

107. BOB DYLAN
00312057 P/V/G $16.99

108. SIMON & GARFUNKEL
00312058 P/V/G $16.99

109. TOP HITS
00312068 P/V/G $14.99

110. JUSTIN BIEBER
00109367 P/V/G $14.99

111. STEVIE WONDER
00312119 P/V/G $14.99

112. JOHNNY CASH
00312156 P/V/G $14.99

113. QUEEN
00312164 P/V/G $14.99

114. MOTOWN
00312176 P/V/G $14.99

115. JOHN DENVER
00312249 P/V/G $14.99

116. JAMIE CULLUM
00312275 P/V/G $14.99

117. ALICIA KEYS
00312306 P/V/G $14.99

118. ADELE
00312307 P/V/G $14.99

119. LADY GAGA
00312308 P/V/G $14.99

120. FANTASIA 2000
00312536 PIANO SOLO $14.99

121. NORAH JONES
00306559 P/V/G $19.99

122. WORSHIP HITS
00312564 P/V/G $14.99

123. CHRIS TOMLIN
00312563 P/V/G $14.99

124. WINTER WONDERLAND
00101872 P/V/G $14.99

125. KATY PERRY
00109373 P/V/G $14.99

126. BRUNO MARS
00123121 P/V/G $14.99

127. STAR WARS
00110282 PIANO SOLO $14.99

128. FROZEN
00126480 P/V/G $14.99

130. WEST SIDE STORY
00130738 P/V/G $14.99

131. THE PIANO GUYS – WONDERS*
00141503 P/V/G $24.99

132. TODAY'S HITS
00147793 P/V/G $14.99

HAL•LEONARD® CORPORATION
7777 W. BLUEMOUND RD. P.O. BOX 13819
MILWAUKEE, WISCONSIN 53213

Visit Hal Leonard Online at
www.halleonard.com

Prices, contents and availability
subject to change without notice.

PEANUTS © United Feature Syndicate, Inc.
Disney characters and artwork © Disney Enterprises, Inc.

* Audio contains backing tracks only.

PLAY PIANO LIKE A PRO!

AMAZING PHRASING – KEYBOARD
50 Ways to Improve Your Improvisational Skills
by Debbie Denke
Amazing Phrasing is for any keyboard player interested in learning how to improvise and how to improve their creative phrasing. This method is divided into three parts: melody, harmony, and rhythm & style. The companion CD contains 44 full-band demos for listening, as well as many play-along examples so you can practice improvising over various musical styles and progressions.
00842030 Book/CD Pack $16.95

BEBOP LICKS FOR PIANO
A Dictionary of Melodic Ideas for Improvisation
by Les Wise
Written for the musician who is interested in acquiring a firm foundation for playing jazz, this unique book/CD pack presents over 800 licks. By building up a vocabulary of these licks, players can connect them together in endless possibilities to form larger phrases and complete solos. The book includes piano notation, and the CD contains helpful note-for-note demos of every lick.
00311854 Book/CD Pack $16.99

BOOGIE WOOGIE FOR BEGINNERS
by Frank Paparelli
A short easy method for learning to play boogie woogie, designed for the beginner and average pianist. Includes: exercises for developing left-hand bass • 25 popular boogie woogie bass patterns • arrangements of "Down the Road a Piece" and "Answer to the Prayer" by well-known pianists • a glossary of musical terms for dynamics, tempo and style.
00120517 .... $9.99

INTROS, ENDINGS & TURNAROUNDS FOR KEYBOARD
Essential Phrases for Swing, Latin, Jazz Waltz, and Blues Styles
by John Valerio
Learn the intros, endings and turnarounds that all of the pros know and use! This new keyboard instruction book by John Valerio covers swing styles, ballads, Latin tunes, jazz waltzes, blues, major and minor keys, vamps and pedal tones, and more.
00290525 .... $12.99

JAZZ PIANO TECHNIQUE
Exercises, Etudes & Ideas for Building Chops
by John Valerio
This one-of-a-kind book applies traditional technique exercises to specific jazz piano needs. Topics include: scales (major, minor, chromatic, pentatonic, etc.), arpeggios (triads, seventh chords, upper structures), finger independence exercises (static position, held notes, Hanon exercises), parallel interval scales and exercises (thirds, fourths, tritones, fifths, sixths, octaves), and more! The CD includes 45 recorded examples.
00312059 Book/CD Pack $19.99

JAZZ PIANO VOICINGS
An Essential Resource for Aspiring Jazz Musicians
by Rob Mullins
The jazz idiom can often appear mysterious and difficult for musicians who were trained to play other types of music. Long-time performer and educator Rob Mullins helps players enter the jazz world by providing voicings that will help the player develop skills in the jazz genre and start sounding professional right away – without years of study! Includes a "Numeric Voicing Chart," chord indexes in all 12 keys, info about what range of the instrument you can play chords in, and a beginning approach to bass lines.
00310914 .... $19.95

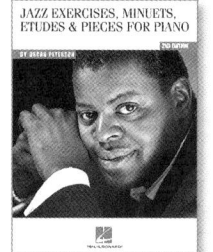

OSCAR PETERSON – JAZZ EXERCISES, MINUETS, ETUDES & PIECES FOR PIANO
Legendary jazz pianist Oscar Peterson has long been devoted to the education of piano students. In this book he offers dozens of pieces designed to empower the student, whether novice or classically trained, with the technique needed to become an accomplished jazz pianist.
00311225 .... $12.99

PIANO AEROBICS
by Wayne Hawkins
Piano Aerobics is a set of exercises that introduces students to many popular styles of music, including jazz, salsa, swing, rock, blues, new age, gospel, stride, and bossa nova. In addition, there is a CD with accompaniment tracks featuring professional musicians playing in those styles.
00311863 Book/CD Pack $19.99

PIANO FITNESS
A Complete Workout
by Mark Harrison
This book will give you a thorough technical workout, while having fun at the same time! The accompanying CD allows you to play along with a rhythm section as you practice your scales, arpeggios, and chords in all keys. Instead of avoiding technique exercises because they seem too tedious or difficult, you'll look forward to playing them. Various voicings and rhythmic settings, which are extremely useful in a variety of pop and jazz styles, are also introduced.
00311995 Book/CD Pack $19.99

THE TOTAL KEYBOARD PLAYER
A Complete Guide to the Sounds, Styles & Sonic Spectrum
by Dave Adler
Do you play the keyboards in your sleep? Do you live for the feel of the keys beneath your fingers? If you answered in the affirmative, then read on, brave musical warrior! All you seek is here: the history, the tricks, the stops, the patches, the plays, the holds, the fingering, the dynamics, the exercises, the magic. Everything you always wanted to know about keyboards, all in one amazing key-centric compendium.
00311977 Book/CD Pack $19.99

HAL•LEONARD®
7777 W. BLUEMOUND RD. P.O. BOX 13819
MILWAUKEE, WISCONSIN 53213
www.halleonard.com

Prices, contents, and availability subject to change without notice.